CORNWALL COUNTY COUNCIL
LIBRARIES AND ARTS DEPARTMENT

'A CORNISH FARMER'S BOY'

by John Tucker

BREWIN BOOKS

First published
by Brewin Books, Studley, Warwickshire, B80 7LG
in month 1993

ISBN 1 85858 023 4

British Library Cataloguing in Publication Data.
A Catalogue record for this book is available from the British Library

Typeset in Plantin by Avon Dataset, Bidford on Avon, Warwickshire, B50 4JH
and made and printed by The Cromwell Press, Broughton Gifford, Melksham, Wiltshire.

This book contains an authentic account of the life, and of the financial achievement of a Cornish farmer's son, spanning the First World War, followed by the financial depression, followed by the Second World War, followed by the affluent era until 1993.

Recording the greatest agricultural revolution ever witnessed, including an authentic account of West Country farming practices, West Country lore, nature in all its forms, an appraisal of the Scriptures relating to creation and to nature in the light of modern experiences.

Written during 1987 by John Tucker.

By Tre, Pol and Pen, ye may know the Cornish men.

The Cornish were descendants of the ancient Celts who had inhabited Western Europe. During recent times many nationalities have left their stamp upon the Celtic race. Every member of the author's family had inherited brown eyes and dark hair. It is believed his family name can be traced back to Roman ancestry.

CONTENTS

John E. Tucker

VOLUME ONE: 1909 – 1955

CHAPTER 1

Farming Family

1909 – 1914

I, John Tucker, was born at Higher Trevollard Farm in the parish of St Stephens-by-Saltash, Cornwall on the afternoon of Tuesday May 4th 1909, being the third of five children born to William and Mary. My sister Winifred born 1905. William (Hedley) born 1906. Myself, then Mary Elizabeth (May) born 1911 and Enid Cordelia born 1915. I was born ten months after the tragic death of Winifred, being conceived and brought into the world while my parents still grieved over the loss of their first born. The crisis and deep grief experienced by my parents vibrated through my infancy impregnating me with a peevish, ill nature.

My mother rocked the cradle in which I lay whenever one of her feet was free to do so with a loving, pacifying motion.

She excused my constant petulance by the fact that her own heavy heart, oppressed by the nagging anxieties and regrets, had transmitted the sadness to her unborn baby.

During my single years I never once saw my mother raise her hand to strike anyone, and I never once heard her raise her voice as a reprimand. A born peacemaker, she never criticised anyone nor did she ever refer to a person's shortcomings.

At the age of eight months and again at the age of eighteen months I contracted what was known then as double pneumonia. Both occasions were severe and could have proved fatal but for my determination to exist. Nevertheless, the results of this illness left me with a weak chest and a persistent cough especially during the desolate night hours when my mother regularly administered comfort with a hot drink, propping up my pillows or encouraging me to sleep in a more comfortable position.

During my teens, a healthy, open air life and my placid nature dispelled all illness, although chesty colds struck me occasionally and I found them more difficult than most lads of my age to shake them off.

My father, William, was born at a Tipwell Farm around 1865. His mother's

My Mother

maiden name was Poad. At an early age he moved with the rest of the family about one mile to occupy the newly built farmhouse at Bealbury Farm, St Mellion which belonged to the Pentillie Estate owned by the Coryton family. My father was born into the Anglican faith and attended St Mellion Church.

There was also a small wayside chapel at Bealbury which my father's family also supported and attended for, during those days it was often an advantage when farming families were members of and supporters of the Anglican Church when tendering for farms owned by the local squire.

My father was the third of twelve children, there were eight boys and four girls. Their names being: Sarah, James, William, Thomas, Hannah, Martyn, Samuel, Edward, Ellen, Edmund, John and a baby girl.

Sarah married William Cox and they had one son John. James married Ellen Veale who were childless. William married Mary Jane Greet and four of their children lived. Thomas married Kate Cox and they had three children: Winifred, John and Edward.

Left to right: Aunt Kate, cousin Winnie, Uncle Tom with Old English Sheepdogs at Gooseford Farm, St. Dominick, 1903

Hannah contracted rheumatic fever from which she did not completely recover. Only Edmund of the remainder married and they were childless. At the present time, it would appear that my two grandsons are the only male survivors from the eight sons of my grandfather who are left to perpetuate the name.

At some period my father and his sister Sarah set up in farming at Torr Farm, Pillaton owned by the Pentillie Estate and my parents married in 1904 when my father was 39 years old.

Torr Farmhouse was situated at the end of a fairly long lane, completely isolated and far from civilisation. My mother refused to marry him to live at Torr Farm so he secured the tenancy of Trevollard Farm, St Stephens-by-Saltash, which adjoins Courtvollard Farm where my mother grew up.

One often speculates why only four of my grandfather's sons married. From experience I can well imagine that it is quite easy to get in a rut especially when finances are low. It is not so attractive facing the prospect of being employed and being ordered around when one has experienced a life of, at least, partial freedom.

While working class children take leaving home in their stride, the self-employed type of farmer's son is more reluctant to do so unless compelled by circumstances.

My two grandfathers died on following days at around the age of 65 years from what sounded very much like pneumonia.

This left two grannies with grown up sons and granny Tucker must have been rather a hard woman. She was the only grandparent that I knew and she lived to the age of 84 years.

One day her younger son came to the kitchen to sit in the corner of the hearth. Gran asked what he was doing there. John told his mother that he had a splitting headache, to which his mother replied, 'We can't have you sitting there doing nothing. I will fetch you some bags to mend'.

Bill Ruse walked two and a half miles each working day from Double Pools, Callington to Bealbury to work a six day week from seven a.m. until six p.m. for thirteen shillings or sixty five pence a week, until one week his wages rose by one shilling to fourteen shillings a week. When on the Saturday Bill went to collect his wages gran said, 'Well, William, I suppose you will expect a rise today.' Bill replied, 'Yes, mam.' Gran grumbled, 'It shouldn't have been allowed.' Bill came back, 'Well, mam, it's the law.' 'Yes' said gran, 'and a purty fine law it is too.'

My mother's father, Thomas Greet, married twice. There were three children from the first marriage. William and Dora survived. It was thought that his first wife died giving birth to the third child. William's two grandsons Gerald and Ron Greet survive at Broadhempston in Devon. Ron Greet in his middle years became involved as a dealer in second-hand tractor parts and today is established as the largest dealer in the country.

Dora married Tom Mason and their daughter Annie married Charlie Crapp. They migrated to Australia around 1923, and they have a daughter Eudora who has a son called Trevor.

Thomas Greet's second wife was Jane Johns, a Dingles (of Plymouth), a shop assistant who had originated from the Launceston area. She produced nine children: Elizabeth, John, Thomas, Mary, Ernest, Mabel, Herbert, Winifred and Stewart. The last two being twins, although Stewart survived but a few days. Thomas Greet had originally worked as a blacksmith at Bull Point, a part of the Royal Naval Dockyard complex at Devonport.

When his second family commenced arriving he said, 'I will not be in a position to give my family much of a start in life on a blacksmith's wage, so I must seek a more lucrative job'. Therefore in the words of the Member of Parliament he 'got on his bike'. He acquired some rented land at Aller Tamerton Foliot where my mother was born and, having given up his job as an Admiralty blacksmith, commenced market gardening and a few years later about 1880 he tendered 395 sovereigns per annum for the tenancy of the seventy odd acres of CourtVollard Farm, St Stephens-by-Saltash which was accepted. For many years the rent was paid in gold sovereigns. At that time it was not considered possible that anyone could pay that amount of money and survive.

Thomas Greet must have been a good manager at home and granny Greet must have been a resourceful saleswoman.

While grandfather Greet stayed at home to produce the goods, granny Greet rose at 3.30 a.m. every Tuesday, Thursday and Saturday to cup cream from the scalded milk, to load the cupped cream, the scalded milk, the home-grown fruit and the light weight vegetables into the spring wagon to catch the first ferry across the Tamar at Saltash to Plymouth market in all weathers, selling the produce on the way. One of the boys took along a chain horse to help the shaft horse pull the wagon up Latchbrook Hill after which he returned home. At that time there was only one human dwelling between the ferry at Saltash Passage and Milehouse, the road actually passing under the G.W.R. line along where the Southern Railway now travels before reaching St Budeaux.

My mother's brother died at the age of 19 years from the effects of a blow from the handles of a horse-drawn plough when the ploughshare struck a stone while working Lower Glebe Field. The cortege at his funeral extended from Roughtor to the top of Latchbrook Hill on the old road and it was one of the longest funeral processions ever seen in the area. John's father had, just prior to this accident, obtained the tenancy of Pengover Farm, Merrymeet for the occupation of John and his sister Elizabeth (Lizzy). This tenancy was cancelled.

My mother attended the private Girls' School of Miss Barnes at Liskeard which was later taken over by Miss Rapson.

My mother lodged over the shop with her cousins, the Snell's family who owned and occupied Snell's Boot Shop in Bay Tree Hill, Liskeard. My mother's brother, Ernest, was educated at Wadham College, Liskeard, and presumably also lodged with the Snell's family in Bay Tree Hill.

When Wiliam Greet married a Miss Rundle, his father set him up as a tenant at Coppadolla Farm situated between Totnes and Newton Abbot. Thomas Greet secured the tenancy of Wadgeworthy Farm near Trematon. Here he set up his son, Thomas and daughter, Lizzy, as tenant farmers. Thomas Greet (junior) later purchased and eventually moved to Latchbrook Farm and never married.

Thomas Greet senior, obtained the tenancy of Penquite Farm near Landrake for Ernest and his wife Nellie, and Ernest later moved to Trehan Farm, Longlands, near Trematon.

Herbert later took over the tenancy of Courtvollard Farm when he married Elizabeth Maddever, and went on to purchase Courtvollard Farm. Thomas Greet senior gave each of his daughters fifty pounds when they married and informed them that this was the best he could do after setting up the boys.

My maternal grandparents had enhanced the social status of their family in a comparatively short period of time through sheer industry and dedication.

My mother was a deeply religious person. She had been brought up in the Non-Conformist Wesleyan Methodist faith and, until she married, acted as Sunday school teacher at Trematon.

She, having raised the largest amount of funds towards the building of the new Chapel at Trematon, was chosen to lay a Foundation Stone and, to mark the occasion, was presented with a delicately shaped silver trowel. At her wedding she was also presented with a handsome Viennese hanging clock from the appreciative congregation of Trematon Chapel.

When she left school granny Greet wanted mother to accompany her to market on Tuesdays, Thursdays and Saturdays. She consented on the condition that she was permitted to learn to play the organ, which she did, and, in due course, played the organ at Trematon Chapel. An American pedal organ was provided at home which gave mother hours of enjoyment for years.

To return to Higher Trevollard Farm and to a tragedy which, although occuring before I was born cast a shadow over much of my life. Prior to the period 1740 when the Land Enclosures Act came into force stone and earth hedges or earth banks had been built to enclose parcels of land in Devon and Cornwall to establish ownership. At this time each parcel of land in the country was measured, recorded and allotted an Ordinance Survey number which was also recorded for, and on behalf of, the National Government, and each measure thus recorded would be a field. Upon these stone, earth or bank hedges were planted Ash, Hazel, Elm, Beech, Thorn, Willow and other species of wood-producing shrubs in order to provide a stock proof fence. Some of these shrubs, Ash in particular, were very fast growing and therefore required very frequent felling. This was accomplished during the winter months when the wood was free from leaves and sap. The small parts of the shrubs, the twigs which were known as spray wood, were cut off and neatly bound in bundles known as faggots. These were collected and built into ricks which were often thatched with reed or straight wheat straw to protect them. This spray wood was used for starting log fires and for heating the cloam ovens which were in every day use baking the meats, bread, cakes, pies or tarts at which my mother was adept. No other form of cooking can produce that exquisite flavour to match food cooked in this way. Cloam ovens were built into the wall by the side of the hearth. The oven itself was round, except for the floor and the door. Its entrance was sealed by this air-tight iron door. Wood faggots were placed inside this oven and set alight when white-hot, the ashes were removed and it was ready for baking. The floor went back three feet and the prepared food would then be placed on this floor and finally the door was closed and sealed. The door remained closed during the cooking process. An experienced cook could gauge the exact temperatures and cooking times perfectly.

Placed near the homestead was usually stored in horizontal heaps the stouter parts of cut wood known as poles to stoke the fires in the hearth and stove. These were split into manageable sized pieces ready for use. It was into the sharp end of one of these poles lying among a pile by the dirt path protruding from the heap, that my sister, Winifred, ran one day at the age of three and a half years when she raced too eagerly to greet her father on his return to the farmhouse to partake of his mid-day meal. Her injuries required surgery but this failed to save her life. She died about a month before I was conceived. Because she was his first born her father had idolised, adored and worshipped her and, perhaps, partly because of the tragic circumstances of her untimely death and perhaps to avoid a repeat of such heart-rending agonising sorrow, my father vowed he would never again permit himself to become sentimentally attached to any of his remaining children. This was a vow my father kept to the letter for the rest of his life. It was even worse than that, he completely ignored us, except for those times when he had work for us to do. Also, at about this time, he had become aware that there was something wrong with his left thigh, which was causing lameness, this knowledge must have caused him a great deal of distress.

On the morning of Tuesday May 4th 1909. I gave due warning of my arrival on this earthly scene. Mother often told of how my father had planned to sow his mangold seed that day. Typical of most farmers and the farming sphere, the sowing of mangold seed or, indeed any operation which affected the farmer's finances, superseded all personal matters. Apparently, after the normal morning milking, the separating of the milk, the feeding of the calves and pigs and the usual farmyard tasks for that period of the year had been completed, my father proceeded to sow his mangold seed.

During that period of his farming career he had competed for prizes by the Hadfields manufacturers of bag fertilizers he had used in growing these crops of potatoes, mangolds, swedes, turnips and cabbages for the highest weights produced per acre.

He had previously won two white, French marble clocks, a barometer, cases of cutlery, teapots, biscuit barrel, flower stands, plaques, etc, which had been suitably inscribed with dates. So, the drilling of all seeds must have of necessity been precise and the right way up. Seeding was therefore time-consuming. It was not surprising that the drilling of the mangold seed had not been completed before the mid-day meal. Instead of my father setting off to collect the midwife from a distance of three miles with the pony and jingle immediately after the mid-day meal, it was necessary for him first to complete the drilling of the mangold seed. By the time he had accomplished this, harnessed the pony to the jingle, driven the three miles to collect the midwife and driven the three miles back, I, being so eager to arrive but, to my mother's consternation, had decided that I was not going to await the arrival of the midwife. Thus it came about that there was only my mother around to smack my

Bushy Sladeland Field, Trewashford
Left to right: My father, brother, James Westington (Jimmy West) and Henry Roseveare of Saltash, Agent for Hadfields fertilisers, Methodist local preacher and friend of the family. Henry Rosevears was a brother-in-law to astronomer John Couch Adams who as a boy was so absorbed in the stars that he turned his father's cows into a field of corn by mistake. With them was Maggie the shire mare holding up a cartload of mangolds
Professor John Couch Adams was the first man to discover the planet Neptune situated almost three billion miles from planet Earth when during 1989 a sattellite sent back pictures to Earth after a journey lasting twelve years

bottom and welcome me into the world. From what I was told later she was even too exhausted to do that and, apparently, I just managed to survive being drowned in my natural surroundings. Fortunately, or unfortunately, depending on the angle from which it is viewed, I survived.

While I can remember being ill when I was very young I cannot relate the illness to any place or any time, by the same token, I have no actual recollection of ever having lived at Trevollard Farm. The family left Trevollard Farm for the 173 acre Trewashford Farm during 1912. The first actual date that I can vividly remember was my fourth birthday which was on a Sunday. I can remember looking forward to attending Pillaton Church of England School on the following morning.

As the years passed and the family grew up our sisters were quite naturally under the influence of a peace-loving, devoted mother and in consequence never put a foot wrong.

However, Hedley and I, being country boys, and full of life were naturally inclined to mischief and delighted in teasing or annoying anyone who permitted themselves to be misled which we often accomplished unchecked.

While memories of incidents which happened at an early age linger, they are of little significance unless dates can be fixed to their happenings. I can remember looking out of a bedroom window at Trewashford on New Year's Day 1914 to see and hear the East Cornwall Pack of foxhounds pursue a fox across five fields belonging to Trewashford Farm. The hounds came in via Higher Kernock Quarry to cross the road, to enter Hilly Sladeland Field, then Bushy Sladeland, cross the road at the bottom, enter Cow Meadow, over a hedge where a gate now stands, enter Square Meadow then cross the lane from Pillaton to Lower Trewashford, cross Long Butters Field, and enter Butters Wood through the gate.

The fox, hounds and the riders were all in view at the same time. I saw the fox enter Butters Wood three fields ahead of the hounds and some of the riders were not far behind. This fox followed the cart track right through the wood to cross the Pillaton Road a couple of hundred yards or so the Pillaton side of Torr Farm entrance gate. The fox crossed another couple of fields before swimming the River Lynher which was in full flood, for Heron Wood and Halwood. The hounds followed the fox across the swollen, fast-flowing river.

Before entering the river on his horse in an attempt to follow the hounds, the Hunt's Whip, Mr Jack Hands, shouted to the others, 'Come on, lads,' but the river was flowing so fast that he soon parted from his horse. Mr Hands grasped and held on to some bushes which hung over the river, while some of the hunt followers galloped their horses to Pillaton Barton Farm where my Uncle Jim farmed at the time, in the hope of obtaining ropes to assist in his rescue. Before these riders returned Mr Hands had been washed away. His body was found three weeks later where it had been left high on a pollard growing by the river bank in the Higher Meadow at Bush Farm when the river dropped. His horse was also found drowned.

My father entered his cowshed on the morning of New Year's Day 1910 while I was lying very ill with pneumonia to discover that during the night one of his milking cows had died from anthrax. My father notified the vets who, in turn, notified the police.

Anthrax, foot and mouth and similar contagious or infectious diseases are notifiable diseases by law, the victims of these diseases automatically become the property of the Ministry and of the Police Authority who are responsible for the disposal of the diseased carcasses. It is usual in such cases for the Authorities to dig deep pits to dispose of the carcasses by burning or burying in lime. My father had been assisting the local Police Officer to dig the pit to bury the anthrax-infected cow. Out of respect for the Officer although he was not actually required to do so when the Police Inspector arrived on the scene and said something to my father which raised his hackles. Whereupon my father said politely to the Inspector, 'I have pressing work which must be attended to. You can take over my job now.' And he immediately downed tools and left the scene.

Some weeks later a knock sounded on the farm door at about eleven p.m. when father had retired for the night. My father opened the bedroom window to enquire the business of the caller, who identified himself as a Police Officer who had arrived to inspect my father's dog license. My father informed him that if he presented himself at the respectable hour of six thirty in the morning he could inspect the license. The Officer was on the doorstep promptly at six thirty a.m. next morning. My father suspected that this Officer had been sent especially by the slighted Inspector.

At about this time a bull became ill at Bush Farm, Pillaton. It was bled by Mr George Lucas who farmed at adjoining Leigh Farm. The animal was dragged into a shed where it was dressed by Mr Vosper, a slaughterman who later became very ill but, after hospital treatment, recovered. I believe I am also right in saying that Mr Lucas at that time had a scratch on his leg which had become infected. He lay ill for a good six months and Doctor Meadows of Saltash treated the infection by applying hot fomentations.

The horse that dragged the bull into the shed died as did some pigs that drank the bull's blood. An employee cut a large chunk of the meat from the rump of the bull and took it home for his wife to cook. She roasted this joint for the family's Sunday dinner. While preparing the meat before roasting it, she cut off a small piece and threw it to Marvel, the household cat, poor Marvel also died.

The employee, his wife and their seven children ate the meal without any ill effects. The cooking of the meat must have been very thorough. While this may be difficult to believe, it was the Gospel truth because that bull had been infected with the deadly anthrax. Since that time, a farm at Trematon lost several cows during a comparatively short period of time from anthrax. These cows often dropped dead in the cattle yard while waiting to be milked. The source of the infection was traced to a small piece of land situated beside a small spring from which it was supposed the animals drank. Had an anthrax victim in the past perchance been buried there? Who knows? It is nevertheless amazing the length of time some diseases can remain infectious and still survive in the soil.

My own recollection of around that era was the sinking of the 'Titanic'. A neighbour, Miss Marks, had told me that Jethro Smith, her friend had missed the train connection which would have taken him to the ill-fated ship. She remembered him cursing vehemently because his horse, for some unknown reason would not leave his stable.

Hedley, May and myself began our schooling at Pillaton Church of England school. The ageing Head Mistress, who taught the older children was called Miss Lucas.

She was a very nice lady who had had the misfortune to receive rather severe burns to her neck when she was young. While probably she was an excellent

Left to right: Mary (May), Hedley and me, 1914

teacher, she had very little command over the maturing country boys who were usually abounding in spirit.

A Miss Clara Dolley was responsible for the education of the younger children. She was the daughter of Sam Dolley who farmed in the village. One afternoon, during the First World War, Eddie Barrett, her soldier sweetheart came in his uniform to the school class room to embrace her before going off to duty. Eddie survived the war, but Clara later married Albert Proctor. They moved to Yealmpton in Devon somewhere around 1924.

Hedley, two and a half years my senior, was a strong, well built boy, and full of mischief. School dinner breaks provided a golden opportunity for terrifying or teasing some poor victim.

Two brothers, Hedley and Harry Cloke, also farmer's sons, of Warren House, with a few village boys including the Dolley brothers from Washing Place, were all tarred with the same brush, these formed the nucleus of the local gang. During those days children and even most adults were obliged to create their own entertainment, which on occasions, could be quite mischievious and mostly at the expense of others.

11

The fields adjoining Pillaton Barton Farm yard on the eastern side are very steep to the valley which extends from Tiddles Well to the river Lynher at Washing Place. One day we boys found a new farm cart wheel belonging to Uncle Jim leaning against a hedge at the top of the steepest hill. Someone set this cart wheel rolling down the slope. As it gathered speed it hit bumps in the field causing it to bounce and the greater the speed the higher it bounced. It eventually bounced into a bog to disappear completely from sight.

Less than a month before writing this I met Harry Dolley at Liskeard Market. Harry was one of the Dolley brothers who had lived at Washing Place which had no approach road as such, probably having been built at some time as a game keeper's cottage and Harry was six or seven years older than me. Our conversation naturally turned to school days. When Harry recalled the affair of the cart wheel. I said, 'Do you remember that?' He said, 'I certainly do. I was there.' Harry died suddenly a couple of days after our chat.

Springing, or setting off, steel rabbit gin traps, during the school mid-day break was a favourite pastime for the young school gang. On one of these forays we must have been observed by our Uncle Jim, for during the afternoon he came to the school to question the boys about some rabbit traps which he had sprung during the dinner breaks. Uncle Jim said it was a boy wearing a red jersey that he had seen springing his traps. Brother Hedley was the only boy in the school who had been wearing a red jersey. Every boy denied springing the traps. Having been the youngest of the gang I was taken apart from the other boys and questioned by my uncle for some time but I insisted that none of our gang were responsible for this misdemeanour. I was about five years old at the time. I was telling a deliberate lie. I knew that I was telling a deliberate lie. I possessed enough sense to realise that Uncle Jim also knew that I was not telling the truth, but at the time I was not prepared to be disloyal to my buddies. It shows how stubborn children can sometimes become when loyalty is at stake, however misplaced that loyalty might be. Young as I then was, that experience taught me a lesson which I never forgot, and which was never repeated. From that time onward I became increasingly aware that one's word is one of the most important factors of one's life, and can usually be construed as a true reflection of a person's trust and character, therefore was determined never to be caught out in a similar situation.

When I was very young, Miss Lucas discovered a packet of cigarettes in Hedley's possession and she sent me home early in the afternoon wth them with the instructions to give them to my father. I cannot recollect being given any written details, I suppose there was a letter, but I do remember waiting between school and home to return the cigarettes to Hedley.

While we never deliberately went 'mitching' from school, we frequently played 'Hares and Hounds' during the mid-day break to arrive back at school late in the afternoon. In spite of this I received a suitably inscribed silver medal presented by the teachers for one year's complete attendance, as, also did May, my sister, which we still possess.

Hedley, as did most of the boys, revelled in teasing and provoking men of an older generation or even any easy-going villager who would fall for their silly tales. My brother was in his element when they became angry or commenced chasing him home. Dan Fowell, whose fields adjoined the school's playground was a frequent victim of the gang's trespassing exploits, and his familiar shout of 'Yer you be again then!' was sweet music to the tormentors.

When Hedley was sent to Callington School the brothers Hedley and Harry Cloke were sent to Plymouth School. They lodged away from our village, and this broke up the gang, at least, as far as school exploits were concerned. When Hedley was either expelled or taken from Pillaton school at around the age of ten years, he was dispatched to a comparatively newly-built Council school in Launceston Road, Callington about four miles from Pillaton. A Headmaster by the name of Mr Arthur Bishop, who was considered very strict, was in command there. Hedley was provided with a pony to ride the four miles to school. I was expelled from Pillaton school by the vicar the Reverend Richard Hocken at the age of nine years. To the dismay of the teachers our parents took May from the school at the same time to send us both to the same Council school in Callington that Hedley was attending. Our parents permitted us to drive their pony and jingle when it was not required to go to market. When it was not available we had to walk the four miles to and from school. As I can so well remember it was quite time that I was moved to another school.

I had been particularly cheeky to Miss Lucas, not for any particular reason because really I liked her. It was pure and simple devilment. I frequently called her 'Old Granny Lucas' to her face when she would quietly reply, 'I am not a granny. If I had children and my children had children, only then would I be a granny. As you must know I have no children, in which case I cannot possibly be a granny.' To which I always replied, 'You are still old granny Lucas to me.' Whereupon I would leave the class room and stroll up the road away from the village to sit in a tree if the weather was kind, to await the school break. This happened often.

Occasionally Miss Lucas would send out older boys with instructions to bring me back but they never succeeded. Two of these boys were the docile brothers Tom and Sam Crago. More than once Miss Lucas told me that the Crago boys were the best behaved boys she had ever taught, whereas the Tucker boys had been the worst.

On one occasion, when Miss Dolley followed me from school into the road while I was slowly walking backwards calling her, 'Old Clara Dolley' among other things I walked straight into the arms of her father old Sam Dolley who at that precise moment happened to have been on his way to one of his fields beyond the school.

Old Sam carried me back into the school and held me in my desk while Clara and

Miss Lucas obtained ropes and bound me securely in my seat to the desk. They kept me there until five o'clock in the evening. This major achievement in all probability made their day.

This state of affairs continued until I was expelled. On the last day at school before Easter after one of my usual walkouts I had returned to the boy's cloakroom to await the school's afternoon dismissal, when the Rector appeared at the cloakroom doorway. He stood there looking toward the school for some minutes before turning around and observing me. As soon as he noticed me he said, 'From now on you are banned from attending this school.'

At a Bethany day school old scholar's re-union held in the British Legion Hall at Tideford during September 1985, which I attended a man approached me and said, 'Hello, John, I can remember when you brought a rabbit to Pillaton School and turned it loose in the class room. Miss Lucas picked you of all the children, Sam Crago and myself to catch this rabbit. How you dived for the rabbit pretending to catch it, and intentionally missing it. You never permitted Sam or me an opportunity to catch that rabbit. It seemed ages before we were able to grasp it firmly.'

I said, 'I don't remember ever turning a rabbit loose in Pillaton School.' He said, 'You did.' I said, 'I don't even remember you.' He said, 'Frank Bennett. We lived at 'Enquire the way' at the time, my sister worked as housemaid for your mother.'

Then I remembered who it was, but it had been a long time since I last saw him, although I had enquired about him earlier that year. At my present age I often wonder why some children are so contrary and so full of mischief. Is it inherited, or is there lack of communication between parents and their offspring?

While my mother and my sisters were very close and, while my sisters were never the cause of annoyance or anxiety to anyone, there was no rapport whatsoever between Hedley and myself with our father. It is a well-known fact, nevertheless, that the youngsters with high spirits, for that is really what it amounts to, are among the nation's most valuable assets. For, given the right direction, and given the opportunity, it will be these same high-spirited youngsters who will be the most likely to pull a nation or a family through a crisis.

Among the many members of the families of Barretts, Battens, Chubbs, Clokes, Dolleys, Frantons, Pearces, Stephens and others who inhabited the village during my schooldays only Charlie Dolley, known to most people those days as 'Noah' and Fernley Cloke, known as 'Captain' survive in the village today. 'Noah' was reared at 'Washing Place' in that family there were: Dick, Tom, Harry, Boxer, Noah, Slugger, Annie, Maud and Beat. A local wag was once reported as having said, 'All my bruvers be called Dick except Tom and he be called Harry.'

At the time when I attended Pillaton School almost all the villagers were employed as manual workers, either in the local workshops or farms. The village then boasted an agricultural implement works owned by Mr John Smale Drown which made good quality farming implements specialising in ploughs, earth cultivators and hay-making machinery including a renowned horse-rake. The premises also contained a 'Smithy' and a carpenter's shop. I have often watched them bind a wooden cart or wagon wheel with an iron rim.

During latter years the carpenter's shop was occupied by Mr John Pearce, with its timber store situated across the road beside the village pound. These last buildings were situated at the entrance to the row of cottages.

The remaining employed persons worked on surrounding farms. Mr William Hawke of Howton and Kernock Farms employed the largest work force to produce vegetables for Plymouth Market on a wholesale basis.

Pillaton Church boasted a peal of six bells which were rung on Sundays and at six o'clock on Christmas morning, also to herald in the New Year. Hymn tunes were often played on the bells on Sundays. As a child the sound of the church bells suddenly ringing down upon me from the tower in the silence of the night and while lying in bed Christmas morning and other specific occasions was to me emotionally inspiring. If there was a pleasure that I missed when we left Trewashford for Molenick at Michaelmas 1925 it was the sound of those church bells. It left a void which has not since been filled.

Since the Second World War Pillaton village has grown considerably. It is now largely occupied by a far more affluent middle-class, collar and tie society.

We arrived home from school one afternoon to find Doctor Davis from Callington and Doctor Meadows from Saltash at the house. At some period during the day Cordelia had become very ill, so ill that father harnessed the pony to the jingle and drove to Callington to fetch Doctor Davis. It happened that Doctor Davis was out on his rounds. Father then drove to Saltash in the hope of obtaining the services of another Doctor. By the time father had returned from Saltash with Doctor Meadows, Doctor Davis had also arrived. The Doctors together examined Cordelia. Their conclusions were that the crisis had passed and that Cordelia had suffered a severe attack of croup and, that, in all probability, our mother had saved Cordelia's life by causing her to vomit.

Mother was advised to keep a bottle of Ipecacuanha Wine handy in the event of a recurrence of the illness. At the time there were no telephones and only a few motor cars. The pony had taken father a round trip of twenty miles to procure the service of this Doctor. Doctors did their country rounds either on horseback, or by a horse and trap in all weathers.

I remember Mr Richard Hancock, a Callington solicitor who was spending a Sunday at our house while on a preaching duty at Pillaton saying, 'They tell us the time is not far off when we will be able to talk with someone in another house many miles away. Soon it won't be safe to speak in our homes without being overheard.'

One Sunday evening when I was about six years old, I put the index finger of my left hand in the wrong place of a treadle sewing machine which Hedley had been idly working. The result was a cut extending the length of my finger which required stitching. My parents took me the seven miles to Saltash in the jingle for Doctor Meadows to stitch. I can still recall the squalling fuss I made before entering Doctor Meadows' surgery.

When I was only a little older, Bert Barrett permitted me to help unload mangolds from a cart to feed the sheep and lambs in Big Whitly Field. Hedley had been sticking a four-pronged fork into the mangolds to lift them over the side of the cart. I was too young to wield a fork so I was using my hands. Hedley went for the same mangold as me. He, accidently plunged one of the four prongs right through the centre of my right hand. The fork emerging in the centre of the palm. That meant another round trip of fourteen miles in the jingle to visit Doctor Meadows. No permanent damage was done.

It was customary for Mrs Dawe of Mushton Farm to take her daughter Leone to Pillaton School on a pony along the same road that we took. Mrs Dawe often gave May a ride on the pony behind Leone. On one of these occasions Mrs Dawe attempted to lift Doreen Fursman of Keason Farm on the pony behind May. The pony objected to this and bolted throwing Leone and May off. In the fall May broke her arm. I had not seen Leone between 1925 and 1980 when, in the vicinity of her home in Kelly Bray, I knocked at her farm door and apologised for bothering her and with a straight face enquired the way to Edgecombe Farm. She, at once commenced to smile and spoke as quietly as she always did when surprised. 'It's John. Isn't it?' I met Doreen Fursman, now Mrs Pearce, a few weeks ago for the first time since 1925.

Headley cut his shin rather badly with a patch hook. At the same time he contracted mild Scarlet Fever, which he passed on to May. As a result she was isolated on the other side of the farmhouse for six weeks.

Chilblains were an affliction from which I suffered greatly as a child during winter and early spring when the flesh on the back of my fingers and thumbs would catch the cold, swell and blister. These blisters broke to become painful, weeping sores. Many times I have gone to school with eight fingers and two thumbs bandaged the full length to cover the open wounds. The irritation when the cold weather relented took some bearing. But strange to tell, being out in all weathers, they only rarely appeared on my feet and toes. Fortunately they disppeared soon after I left school. Although I was plagued with hard 'chaps' later, but this was the usual nuisance for outdoor workers.

The First World War dominated my early years as it dominated the lives of every person in the country. Before the war father always employed two or three regular workers. Jim or Jimmy West had, on leaving school, come to work on the farm and lived in the house as one of the family. Jim volunteered for military service not long after the outbreak of the First World War. He wrote home to us a few times sending a photograph of himself in uniform. And at Christmas time he sent an old-style

James Westington

Christmas card together with a silk handkerchief for May which she still treasures. He disappeared completely for four years. It eventually transpired tht he had spent those four years in Mesopotania. Now known as Iraq.

It was quite some little time after the war ended that Miss Alma Chubb, who was working in the farmhouse at the time, rose at daybreak one summer morning during 1919 to harness the pony to the jingle in order to convey the cans of Cornish cream to Hatt for collection by the dairyman. As soon as Alma opened the back door of the farmhouse which faced the cattleyard, across the uneven slabbed yard she observed a scraggy, unkempt dishevelled soldier emerge from the hayhouse. She let out a cry, ran to the bottom of the front stairs and shouted in alarm, 'Missis, missis!' Mother sensing Alma's alarm called down, 'What's the matter, Alma.' To which Alma's quietened voice answered, 'It's alright.' It had dawned on her by now that the poor soldier was Jim West who had returned home overnight. He had left Trewashford Farm a strong, healthy, young man who was always completely unaffected by outdoor work. Afterwards he developed asthma, over the years this progressively

Trewashford Farm House

worsened causing him considerable distress. I have known father to send Hedley to Callington in the early hours of the morning to fetch Doctor Davis to attend to the poor lad, who would be literally gasping for breath. Doctor Davis told Hedley once that there was very little he could do for Jim saying, 'In any case asthma will not kill anyone.' Jim died from cancer at the age of fifty four. He was never awarded a disability pension. Over the years I have felt guilty that my parents had not applied to get some compensation for Jim. Many years later we learned that he had specifically requested his wife not to apply. As a country we are far from generous to subjects and dependents who have made such killing sacrifices both physical and mental.

When we moved to Molenick from Trewashford at Michaelmas 1925 Jim stayed in Pillaton to marry Maude Dolley of Washing Place. There were two sons of the marriage. The eldest became an engine driver for the G. W. R. We visited him many times as he settled down to a happy family life.

Peter Barratt, an older man, who had been working for father on the farm when the war started left father to work on the roads for the council. Last year Tom

'A CORNISH FARMER'S BOY'

A story in two volumes: 1909 – 1993

Dedication

I dedicate this book to my parents, to whom I owe my existence. My family has been blessed with loyal, devoted, unselfish women folk. I wish to name especially: Granny Greet; my mother; my sister, May; my wife, Evelyn; and our daughter Mary. Their placid caring nature has earned them the respect of all with whom they came in contact. More than a half of whatever their menfolk have achieved is due to their devotion.

At the ceremony of the unveiling of Pillaton Memorial, erected in honour and in memory of the fallen of the 1914–1918 War. Standing together on the left nearest camera was my father and Mr Tom Crags, standing alone in front of them was County Alderman William Hawke.
Addressing the ceremony was Lt. Col. W. P. Drury. The Rector, Mr Richard Holken stood on his right with hand to ear.

Pearce told me that Arthur Chubb had also worked for my father before he enlisted. He had put his age forward in order to get accepted. I remember well talking to Arthur one Sunday afternoon when I was returning home from Sunday school. He was sitting in a roadside hedge belonging to Trewashford Farm. On the following day he left home to rejoin his unit. The following Monday his mother received notification that he had been killed in action.

There was also the youngest son of Farmer Pearce from Rowse, situated near Pillaton village and almost adjoining our place at Trewashford Farm, he had rejoined his unit with Arthur on the Monday and was killed in action the same day.

The reasons for this war soon became lost in the bloody holocaust when lives of men became more expendable than lives of horses. Even at an early age the war was influencing our everyday living. Our approach to the future had lost much of the fire and ambition amidst the awful uncertainty of which loved one would be lost next. The political and military leaders on both sides of the conflict must have been crazy for power to have ordered wave after wave of their country's manhood into battle against such over- whelming conditions to satisfy their accursed egoism. The war at sea was equally inhuman and cruelly mismanaged.

The war eventually ended in stalemate when the opposing enemies were all facing starvation. It had not been realised until the British and Allied prisoners of war began returning to homes and homelands how near that the Germans had come to starvation.

When these prisoners of war returned to home ports they were so emaciated that some of their own relations were unable to recognise them. However obscure the cause of the First World War, there was no winner. Bitterness had been engendered to produce one more reason for the Second World War. Had Britain and her Allies definitely held the Western Front instead of sending so many gallant men into battle merely to provide machine gun fodder it would have prevented nine tenths of the Allied casualties. It would also have released sufficient labour to have produced enough food for our troops and our civilian population to have starved the enemy into submission. This, unfortunately, would not of itself have prevented a Second World War.

Pillaton Church of England School certainly taught us the virtues of patriotism. A photograph of Jack Cornwall, a very brave young man, a mere boy, who had sacrificed his life for the cause and country was presented to each pupil to emulate and to honour. We were told that God was on our side in the struggle that was being waged to end all wars. What a blinder! After the war each little community, usually through the Parish Council, set about erecting its memorial in honour, and in memory, of the fallen.

Pillaton was one such community and the Parish Council set about arranging and financing the project. County Alderman, William Hawke of Kernock Farm, I believe, was the leader of the committee and my father was also a member. The finances for the memorial were duly provided. The memorial stone itself had been ordered, the position for its erection had been settled, and plans for the unveiling were being discussed. It was decided that, weather permitting, the memorial service would be held at the foot of the memorial. The next decision to be taken was what should happen if the weather did not permit. Whereupon the tall figure of the Rector of Pillaton Church, the Reverend Richard Hocken, who was very deaf, rose high on his toes, as was his wont, cupped a hand over his ear, and said, 'When I was ordained to this church, I vowed that no Non-Conformist Minister would ever be permitted by me to enter my pulpit while I am in charge of this church. That vow still stands. If there are any Non-Conformists taking part in the memorial service, I cannot permit the service to be held in my church.' How these Christians loved one another.

This, then, was the war that was fought so dearly to end all wars. This was the war when God was wholly on our side. What a farce! Fortunately the weather permitted the service to be held at the foot of the memorial.

Although the First World War was being fought on the other side of the English Channel, the experience of seeing Eddie Barrett enter the school class room in uniform, with his pack, to tearfully embrace his school-teacher sweetheart on his way to the battle front, the loss of Arthur Chubb and many other boys of the Parish that we had all known so well; seeing the return home of the emaciated prisoners of war and hearing first hand accounts of the terrible experiences of the soldiers returning from the trenches, all these facts left deep scars on the memory of the young people on this side of the English Channel.

Alma Chubb, as already mentioned, had come to live at our farm around the middle war years, she was a very capable girl, well-liked and respected and became one of the family. She was Arthur Chubb's sister. One Sunday afternoon, on returning home from Sunday school a flock of sheep met us on the road by Trewashford Farm. The ram from the flock left his ewes to chase me, I having been some distance from the others. I climbed on top of, and sat on some gates against the cow house wall. Alma following behind had seen my predicament, and assuming that the sheep belonged to the farm, she climbed over the hedge and opened the gate to Long Sladeland Field, and turned them in with our sheep. After the straying sheep had entered the field Alma shut the gate. I removed myself from my safe position and walked to the field gate to peer through the bars at the sheep. I saw two sheep begin to fight and it wasn't long before one ram rolled over with a broken neck. I ran indoors to where a Mr John Paynter, the preacher for the day, who was an uncle of my father, and also a farmer, was reclining in the lounge. I endeavoured, but failed, to interest Mr Paynter in the affair. I then proceeded to the cowshed where father was milking the cows. I explained the situation to him. He did not visit the field, instead he sent me to Mushton Farm to tell Mr Dawe what had happened. I must have explained the details sufficiently well for my father to have understood that it was Mr Dawe's ram which had received the broken neck. The carcase would have been edible had it been bled.

A caring girl, Alma, one evening picked up and brought home three young tawny owls which she had discovered at the foot of a tree on the way back to Lower Trewashford via the Quarry route. She kept and fed these owls in the large mealhouse-cum-washhouse where a window was always left open to provide access for the farm cats. At the time there was a family of cats, more than half grown, living in this mealhouse. During the night two of these young cats had been violently killed by something, we couldn't understand what it was but the young owls were unharmed. At the time we wondered if the parent owls had delivered the fatal blows to the cats. Tawny owls still frequent Trewashford Farmhouse where they are sometimes found in the living rooms having entered via the wide chimney. They are handsome birds with their beige and golden colouring. It can now be claimed that in all probability the owls would have survived had they been left in the shelter of the tree roots.

Years later, Alma joined her fiance Arthur Cloke, brother of Hedley and Harry, in New Zealand. Their descendants now reside in the city of Invercargill, South Island, the southernmost city in the world. By the time the First World War had been in progress for a couple of years the powers that were began to realise that the war was not likely to end quickly. Both sides had thrown masses of troops at the enemy guns, and up until now, the guns had won. It was becoming increasingly apparent that food, or lack of food, could well influence the result of the war.

Soldiers who had been under severe stress in the front line were drafted to farms for a short period as a break. A Canadian soldier by the name of Oates was billeted with my parents during one early Autumn. He was a man who had possessed considerable farming experience, being very capable and efficient. He was far more valuable to the war effort producing food than as cannon or machine gun fodder in the battle zone. He was with us for a couple of months when he reluctantly left the farm that was the end, we never heard from him again. A British soldier was the second from one of the towns in the North of England to be sent to us, he also stayed for a couple of months. His name was Fennel Rapier. Fennel carried a shattered Bible in his tunic breast pocket which had diverted an enemy bullet. Fennel had possessed no farming experience but being a willing and intelligent man adapted to the new way of life admirably.

After Fennel a Cornish gypsy by the name of William Cooper helped us on the farm and he stayed for a much longer period of time than the two previous men. He married locally and settled down in a caravan with his wife and two children at Callington. For some time before the end of the war German prisoners were stationed at Compton Hall, Callington and at Amy down near Amy Tree where six roads converged. These prisoners of war were available to farmers for harvest work under guard. They helped father with the corn harvest of 1918. These soldiers were tall Prussian Guards, the ground fairly shook when they jumped down from the top of a wagon load of corn sheaves. While Hedley and me were warned not to give them food we could not resist collecting and presenting them with new-laid hen's eggs which we watched them swallow raw.

Quite recently a fine car, driven by a lady, pulled up outside the home of Mr and Mrs George Gregory (Trewartha Gregory and Doidge Ltd. Callington) to enquire where the First World War German prisoner of war camp had been situated as her ageing father, seated in the car, wished to visit the site where he had been held prisoner of war. Mr George Gregory said, 'You have come to the right place for this information. As a boy I was friendly with one of the camp guards and visited the camp often playing cards or football.'

It proved to be a very emotional return after all those years. George Gregory who is two years older than me lived at Trewashford Farm before we moved in. My father claimed he was the first to cut young George's hair, and what a tantrum he set up. The British public had not been aware at the time of the signing of the

Armistice that the war had been brought to an end through lack of food. That awareness did not come about until our men returned to Britain weak from lack of nourishment. Britain was facing hunger, but Germany was facing starvation when the Armistice was signed. The war had reached a stalemate on land, because both war machines were bogged down in spite of the tragic, unnecessary, unavailing destruction of the cream of our young manhood. Britain and the Allies could have achieved the same results with one tenth of the casualties had Britain maintained a defensive stance only, throughout the war period. But that is hindsight.

Nevertheless, military intelligence must have been non-existent for the military leaders and their advisors to have sacrificed the lives of so many for so little. The horrific tragedy was that in spite of the terrible carnage, the First World War remained unfinished according to first hand opinions of the British Tommy so often expressed to me between the wars.

CHAPTER 2

Feeding the Home Front

1914 – 1918

The owner of Trewashford Farm, when my father took over the tenancy in 1912, was a Mr Digby Collins of Newton Ferrers, a country mansion with an agricultural estate attached, extending to something over 2,000 acres.

On the death of Mr Digby Collins, his nephew, Mr Thurston Collins, inherited the estate to become the landlord and local squire. The game on the estate was reserved by the landlord. On account of the war no gamekeeper was employed. When the occasional pheasant shoot took place, tenants or their sons would 'Brush' or 'Flush' the game birds for the guns. Shoots were held on Saturdays when boys were home from school and would commence about 10.30 a.m. Hedley and I represented our father at these shoots. Refreshments were provided between 1 and 2 p.m. when the only liquid refreshments provided was beer and cider. As a young schoolboy when assisting at one of these shoots on a very hot autumn day I became parched by lunch time when I must have over indulged in the refreshment room.

As the afternoon progressed so did a splitting headache. I managed to last the afternoon, but only just. I did feel ill. Hedley, two and a half years my senior, was physically stronger and presumably, much wiser. Anyway if I was drunk on that occasion I have never·become drunk since, for the limit of my alcohol consumption has never exceeded one half pint of lemonade shandy a year. This has not been because I signed the pledge, it is simply because I had no money to form the habit during my thirty years of age.

From a very early age farmer's sons were encouraged, even required to destroy vermin by whatever means were at their disposal to protect the farmer's crops and to protect his landlord's game. Vermin in those days included: rats, moles, rabbits, magpies, crows, stoats, when they killed chickens and foxes and badgers when they killed geese. While the only safe way to kill a rat is to club it to death, I have often caught hold of their tails at the times when they permitted their tails to betray their presence by leaving them trailing outside their holes, and pulled them out fast to swing them against a wall. These methods might not be an appropriate subject for a religious prayer meeting held for the sophisticated, civilised society, or for the squeamish. It is, however, a fact of life which farmer's boys have to face and come to

25

terms with. Ricks of corn which were left to stand for a while before being threshed usually contained several rats and mice. With the aid of dogs and sticks as many as possible were gleefully destroyed as if it were a sport.

During the First World War May and I caught moles in traps, skinned them and tacked their skins on a board to dry. When dry they were sold for up to as much as a shilling a skin. We were permitted to keep the money we received for these skins. Rabbits also abounded on almost every farm in those days. To conserve game for the landlord, tenants ferreted as many rabbits as time would permit. Steel gin traps were used only as a last resort. Hedley and I commenced ferreting rabbits as soon as we were able to handle a ferret, set up nets and break the neck of a rabbit. Any spare time during the autumn and winter months that was left after the cattle, sheep, pigs and horses had been fed and attended to, we spent rabbiting, that is, apart from Sundays. Fortunately we kept an old English Sheep Dog terrier bitch which was a Jill-of-all-Trades. She worked cattle and sheep, she would keep the rooks off the corn, she was a good guard dog, and especially clever when we took her into the woods where the ground sets, as opposed to the hedge or bank sets, there she would mark rabbits unerringly when they were at home. If the rabbit lay deep in the burrow, she would commence digging with her paws. If the rabbit was close inside the entrance to the burrow she would look into the hole, moving her head first to one side then the other repeating the action but refraining from digging. It was a waste of time setting up nets and putting the ferret into the rabbit set had she not firstly marked the rabbit at home. Nothing pleased Hedley and me more than to sneak into someone else's wood with this bitch, a ferret and a few nets when rabbits were 'bolting' well, which didn't happen always, and to emerge with a bag full of rabbits. When ferreting our home territory, we invariably hung rabbits up to cool as soon as they had been caught, it would not have been prudent to have done this on a neighbour's property.

One day we entered Butters Wood through the hedge, some distance below the gateway where the fox had been chased by the eager Mr Hands and his fellow huntsmen on that fateful New Year's Day in 1914. Hedley, as usual, led the way. We had travelled into the wood some distance when Hedley turned around to retrace his steps. When drawing alongside he whispered, 'Frank.' Regarding this as just another of his pranks I continued on my way. Very soon I came face to face with 'Frank' who just looked straight at me saying nothing. This wood belonged to Frank Pearce. I turned slowly around and followed Hedley from the wood. In all probability, had we asked Mr Pearce if we could ferret rabbits in his wood he would have said, 'Yes,' willingly, for we had always been good friends. In the event we were trespassing and we knew this. It was quite possible that Mr Pearce had told our father what had happened and both had a quiet chuckle at our hasty retreat. This happened during the First World War when I was about seven years old.

Only within this last month I learned that Frank Pearce is a distant relative by marriage. Frank had married Leah Hill, and my wife's eldest step-brother had married Frank's sister-in-law.

This same Leah Hill had worked for my Aunt Ellen at Pillaton Barton before she married Frank. She once asked for an evening off to which Aunt Ellen replied, 'Well, I'm not sure if you can, Leah. You must realise it is harvest time just now.' To this refusal Leah grumbled, 'It's harvest time all the year round here, mam.'

By the door of the pump house at Trewashford Farm was a cat-flap. When I was at a loose end I would set up a rabbit net outside this hole and drive one of the farm cats through it, whereupon the bewildered creature became enveloped in the net strings. The fun was not altogether in rolling it up in the net, but disentangling the frightened cat quickly while avoiding its bites and scratches from the needle-sharp claws.

My father had once caught seven rabbits in a short space of time with a steel gin trap set in a small hole in a hedge near the homestead. I could do nothing better than to put my fingers in this trap. I was too small to release my fingers from its jaws so, I pulled up the stake securing the steel trap and proceeded squalling past the steaming dung heaps, to my mother who was milking the cows in the byre.

Not long after this I was walking with May along by, and inside, the top road hedge of Long Sladeland Field when I said to her, 'A rabbit trap is set there.' She said indifferently, 'Where?'

'There.'

She answered 'There's not.'

'There is.'

'There's not.'

'There is.'

'There's not.'

I tried to prove I was right by further arguing, 'All right then. Put your fingers in. Then you will believe me.' She put her fingers in the contraption and 'bang' went the gin. After I prised open its teeth to set her fingers free I begged her, 'Tell your mother you fell off the hedge.'

A few years ago I visited Bill and Sid Jane at Dunnerdake Cottages. Sid's grandson who lived in the farmhouse was with him. Sid said to me, 'John, my grandson is crazy about rabbiting. I have been explaining some of our past escapades when out in the fields. Without exaggerating, I've told him of the vast number of rabbits we encountered and with which we were plagued before myxomatosis. He won't believe a word I say.' Sid added. 'Can you convince him that what I've told him is true?'

I confirmed to Sid's grandson, 'Young man, rabbits were so thick and plentiful. When we were young they were often seen queueing up to enter their holes and it was not uncommon when we went ferreting to have to pull half a dozen rabbits out of a hole before there was room to put the ferret away.' Sid gazed at his grandson with a straight face and winking at me told him, 'There, boy, what have I been telling you all along.' Rabbits 'bolted' from the ferrets far better on some days than they did on others, depending mostly on the weather conditions. Rabbits detested east winds and just would not move. This was when the lie-ups occurred, when the ferrets ate out the timid rabbit's eyes. Like horses, rabbits were more frisky and lively when the wind came strong from the south or west. Rabbits were dispatched instantly and humanely when their necks were dislocated and, when the need arose, I have dispatched cats, as well as fair sized puppies, in this manner. One of the severest frosts this century occurred during the early months of 1916, when millions of British, Commonwealth, allied and enemy troops suffered unspeakable hardships in the Flanders trenches. Here, at home, the frosts were followed by a long cold, wet period producing even more merciless conditions for the farm animals.

The mangolds rotted in their clamps, and swedes rotted in the ground where they had grown. There was not sufficient workers on the farms or the facilities, with which to cope, in feeding corn to the animals. There was no machinery available for bruising corn, there was no adequate manger or trough space to feed the available food to the animals, or replace the lost mangolds and swedes.

The army had commandeered all of father's best hay for the army horses. Cattle was fed on straw. Many of the young cattle died from starvation during the month of May 1916. For a while the young cattle were fed as much straw as they would eat, but it took more nutrients than the straw possessed to digest this course food, which meant, quite simply, that if only straw was their main diet for any length of time, the animals would, inevitably die from starvation. This is what precisely did happen that dreadful springtime.

A phrase, fortunately not heard these days, but often very meaningful in those far-off days, was, 'While March may search, and April try, May is the month that cattle die.'

The stomachs of the starving cattle were unable to accommodate or to withstand the richness of the young May grass. That was the lesson that I learned the 'hard way' as a child at the expense of my father and neighbouring farmers. Later, when cattle came into my care, they were all fed home-grown cereals during the winter months. Home-grown cereals have always been the cheapest food to feed to animals. No animal has ever died from starvation while in my care.

A relevant story has often been told, which, when taken literally, will make considerable sense. An old lady at market one spring attending a sale presented cattle which were looking extremely fit and well. A prospective buyer when looking over these cattle remarked to the old lady, 'Your cattle are looking remarkably well, missis. What have you been feeding them on to get them in that condition?' To which she replied, 'All they have had to eat is a bit of straw and that wasn't half-threshed.' As part of their daily winter ration cereals have always been the cheapest form of feeding sheep and cattle, especially if it home-grown. Cereals may now even compete with modern-made silage. During the spring of 1916 not a single ewe produced a sufficient amount of milk to rear more than one lamb on my father's farm. From ewes that produced more than one lamb only one of the multiple births survived. At the present time we are geared to feed cereals to ewes whatever the weather conditions.

The autumn of 1917 must have been one of the wettest of the century. Lack of harvest workers might have made it appear worse than it really was. When Mr Martin, the tenant of Newton Ferrers Barton left the farm at Michaelmas 1917 the corn had been cut with a binder and stitched, stooked or stocked. This meant standing sheaves on their butt ends in wind rows three or four sheaves standing on their butt ends leaning against the exact number standing the same way on the opposite side with the wind blowing through the centre. Occasionally there would be seven or nine sheaves with one sheaf standing in the centre and the six or eight standing against the centre sheaf. This stook could be thatched by placing another sheaf upside down and around the top of the stook. This was known as 'hatting'. A good crop of wheat neatly stooked and 'hatted' produced an inspiring sight, a portrait of good farming industry. Only enough sheaves were carried to half-build one rick before Newton Ferrers Barton Farm clearance sale took place, a few days before Michaelmas 1917. At this sale Mr Martin sold his entire live and dead farm stock including the horses and wagons. He also offered corn for sale by the field as it stood in stooks. Mr John Cox, the ingoing tenant, bought two of these fields of corn and carried and threshed the corn straight from the field on Boxing Day and the following day. My father also carried a field of corn on the same Boxing Day, this field was called Lower Down at Lower Trewashford.

I well remember to this day making some of these loads of corn for my father. I was eight years old. Thistles grew profusely among the corn and in the clear threads of pleasant memories, I can see Alma at harvest time sitting in the fields waiting for the next wagon to arrive, as she carefully removed the thistles from my fingers and arms.

It was at Newton Barton Farm that what might have been a serious accident occurred before the advent of electricity. Three workers were clipping a shire horse one evening after dark. One man was turning the handle of the clipping machine, one man was clipping the horse and the other worker held a naked candle to enable the man handling the clippers to watch his movements. Everything was proceeding normally until the clipping reached the horse's rear end. The man holding the naked candle was standing immediately behind the horse when the horse broke wind and the candle ignited the escaping gases. There followed an almighty explosion. This naturally frightened the horse, which immediately kicked out and struck the poor man who had been holding the flaming candle sending him flying through the open door into the stable yard.

It was during the summer at around this period that Hedley was sent by father one evening to inspect some sheep in Higher Down Field at Lower Trewashford. This field was one of the farthest from the homestead.

Hedley left home with the fullest intention of inspecting these sheep but on the way met some boys of his own age group and whether he forgot his mission or not, I cannot recall. He had obviously failed in his promise because the following day father found that one of them had been eaten alive with maggots, or if it wasn't dead when father found the animal, there was so much damage done that it never recovered. There was hell to pay over this for had Hedley carried out his father's instructions the previous evening he would have observed the sheep's condition and it may have been saved. Everyone of the family was in the doghouse because of this needless loss. Great care had always been the rule in our household to prevent such a nasty thing to happen, but things will go wrong on occasions even in the most regulated households.

Fortunately, for the shepherd and for the sheep we are now able to dip sheep with a powerful maggot fly repellant twice during the summer months. This fly repellant will discourage the maggot fly, the bluebottle, from laying its eggs in the sheep's wool, or should it manage to lay its eggs there, this strong liquid will prevent the eggs from maturing. There was nothing available in pre-war days on a commercial basis to prevent the loss of valuable animals in this painful way. It is often difficult to detect maggots in sheep especially close-woolled breeds and sheep can sometimes become infested with maggots without showing visible signs, apart from the actions of the infected animals. Late one autumn evening I moved fields with a fairly large flock. All appeared well until the ewes moved out into the field, when I noticed one of the Suffolk rams which had been running with the flock suddenly lie down. This was unusual I caught this ram and on examination found to my horror that it was pickled with young maggots and fly-blows. There was no sign of a stain on his wool, but he would not have survived had he received no attention for a further twenty four hours.

Yesterday morning I witnessed yet another of nature's all too frequent tragedies. At 10.30 a.m. a passing motorist called in at the farm to inform one of our staff that he had seen a sheep being attacked by many birds in a field next to the road. I took my car and travelled in the direction from which the motorist came to search for the sheep he had seen in trouble. I drove almost a mile with my eyes skinned but saw nothing. On the return journey I saw the sight that had caused the gentleman to stop. A ewe which had rolled onto her back had been unable to right herself. She was in one of Richard Baker's fields. Birds had punctured her belly by one of her flanks. Her entrails were strewn across half an acre of the field. Her belly was covered in the reddest of blood and the birds had also eaten out her eyes. She was still alive, so I placed her in a sitting position. Mr Baker went up to the field soon after and shot her to put her out of her misery. The birds concerned were ravens, black-backed gulls, crows and one buzzard. I drove to the Baker's farm where

Richard's son told me that the sheep had been inspected earlier that morning.

These happenings strangely do not prevent us from singing and believing that all thing are bright and beautiful, wise and wonderful and the the Lord God made all things great and small: predators and non-predators.

What had made matters more difficult during the first war years was the fact that our father was becoming more lame in his left leg. In consequence, he needed the assistance of a walking stick which he always used when working a team of horses in the fields. Considering the work to be carried out daily such as: cows to milk, milk to separate, cream to scald, butter to make, calves to be fed either with milk or cereals, mangolds or hay. Young and older cattle to be fed with hay, straw, mangolds or turnips. Sheep to feed and shear. Fields to plough, weed and harvest. Animals to bed down and house. Mucking out, and the manure to be taken to the fields and spread by hand. Horses to be fed and groomed. Rabbits to be kept under control. It was a crazy, unsound situation when one crippled man was left to cultivate 173 acres to produce food for man and horses on the war front and to satisfy the hungry open mouths of the millions of humans on the home front. This meant that our mother often helped to milk cows, make butter, feed and rear poultry, collected and washed the eggs, fed the family and ran a large, cold, draughty farmhouse, more often than not without help. It also meant that Hedley and I was roped in to all manner of farm jobs at a very early age. I was taught to milk when I was about five years old. We would be given the task to milk an old dairy cow that had not much milk to give. It wasn't long before I was sent out to check up on the health of the sheep, or move them into different fields to graze.

While father possessed a dog which would work sheep for him, that dog would not work sheep for me. This created problems and made the work so hard for a young boy.

As soon as we were strong enough to control horses we were put in charge of a team to work on Saturdays also during spring and summer holidays. There were times when I became a little scared that I could not control some fractious, young horses. They knew when you drove them around the headland of the field it was a sign that the work was almost completed, they would then take the bit between their teeth to sail around the field at speed. Fortunately they knew enough to stop when they reached the entrance gate. It caused me many anxious moments.

Horses were never worked on Sundays. These special rest days when the weather was warm and dry they could be seen lying stretched flat out on the ground in the fields. These were the only days working horses would be seen lying around in this manner, as if they knew it was their day off.

During April and May each year father would chain harrow the grass fields which were intended for making hay. The chain harrow loosened the stones and also provided a marker guide which could be followed by May and myself when collecting the loosened stones and the trash which was put into buckets to prevent them blunting the mower knife. This was a soul-destroying job for young children, meal times always seemed ages away. We absolutely loathed this farm chore.

Hedley was a strong boy, two and a half years my senior, who often did a man's job at a very early age. It often happened that on dry week-day evenings during the summer months father would take Hedley and me to the sheep field. The dog would collect the sheep and keep them in a corner while Hedley and me caught the lame sheep and turned them into a sitting position to help father trim their overgrown hooves, and to apply Butter of Antimony with a chicken wing feather to the parts of the sheep's feet affected with foot rot or stripped between the claws. Every evening during the winter months when the cattle and horses were housed, Hedley and I went the rounds after eight o'clock to feed the cows, horses and sheep. If it was lambing time, it was my duty to carry the hurricane lantern while Hedley did the haying and corning up, or bedding down of the cattle and horses and to generally observe their welfare.

Experience soon taught us to reasonably predict the time when a cow or mare would give birth to their offspring. This often led to visits to the byre during the night to confirm the safe arrival of the newly born or to render assistance. When everything is normal a mare will deliver her foal very quickly, for she strongly objects to delivering her foal when humans are in attendance. She will deliberately wait until humans have turned their backs before delivering her young one. We have often worked mares in low harness traces, right up until they have foaled. I remember as recently as 1939 working a pregnant mare the whole of one morning and on returning to the stable after a short mid-day break to find her foal standing strongly and suckling with the mare feeding normally. If a working mare is being regularly fed with corn when pregnant the foal at a very early stage will kick every time the mare commences to eat the corn, or to take a drink. Close observation will detect this shudder along the mare's flanks and side. Extra teeth grow on either side of the mouth of a male horse. At the age of nine years, when not at school, I was in charge of my father's seventy plus flock of ewes at lambing time. I visited a field called Big Whitly very early one Sunday morning to discover that a South Devon ewe had given birth to four strong, even-sized lambs. This in itself was not unusual. What was unusual in those days was the fact that this ewe reared them all reasonably well by herself, without her lambs receiving any assistance. I brought this ewe with her four lambs and another ewe with three lambs, also a ewe with two lambs from their daytime field to the shelter of a house every evening where I fed the ewes with corn and mangold. I returned them to the field the following morning before leaving for school. We still possess photographs of this ewe with her four lambs with myself proudly holding the mother.

Looking at the photographs one day I said to my mother, 'Fancy dressing up in clothes like that.' Some time later I asked her, 'Why haven't I seen the photos of the lambs lately?' She replied, 'Because you won't.' Again I pressed her, 'Why not?' She

John holding South Devon ewe with four lambs she bred unaided during 1918.
John Tucker. Age 9
Loose Cover and inside page, vol one

just said quietly, 'I put them on the fire.' The photos we now have came from Auntie Lizzie.

During the first war period the number of South Devon cattle kept on the Trewashford Farm was around eighty about twenty of which were cows producing calves and milk.

The calves were reared on milk which had been separated from its cream. Calves which were not required for herd replacements were kept until fully grown to be fattened for beef or sold as forward stores. During these days the use of compound bag fertilisers was confined to cereals, root crops and to fields intended for hay. Basic slag superphosphates sufficed from grazing land, no straight nitrogen fertiliser was sown on grazing land. The milk produced was put through a machine which was known as a cream separator. The machine extracted more cream from the milk than did the old scalding process and far more labour saving. The cream separator was turned by hand, but could also have been operated by an engine. The separated cream was first left to cool, it was then scalded, then cooled and left to ripen in the dairy. The cream could then have been placed in a butter churn, when the churn could have been revolved until it turned into butter, but my mother turned the cream into butter by hand, it saved so many utensils.

The operation, nevertheless, required much labour. It meant placing the cream into a butter tub, turning, kneading and patting by hand for quite some time until the cream thickened then curdled. As it continued to curdle, the milk remaining from the cream stage separated from the butter, this was sold as buttermilk. When all the milk had been extracted salt was added both to improve the flavour and to preserve it. A contrivance rarely used was the butter dolley worked with the butter tub. It consisted of a flat cover which locked into the handles of the tub. Through a hole in the centre of the cover a handle on the top connected with paddles in the form of a fan underneath the cover to turn the cream into a delicious butter. Anyone free in the home could take turns with the handle.

This process proved more arduous in hot, sultry or thundery weather. During such periods I have known our mother to rise very early in the morning to recover pans of cream from the butter well where they had cooled overnight. Benches were built around the walls of the well from thick slabs of the cool Delabole slate on which to rest the huge pans of cream. There was a similar well built at the bottom of Long Sladeland Field at Trewashford. The farmhouse dairy was invariably built at the North East corner of the ground floor, with windows facing North and East and with Delabole slate covering the entire floor. A table in the centre, also benches around all four walls was formed from the same Delabole stone. The windows which were normally left open, were completely enclosed with fine metal gauze to exclude the smallest fly. The room was always cool and airy from these shaded windows.

My mother weighed the butter into pounds and smaller packs. These she placed on round moulds the imprint of which displayed the weight and my father's name together with a thistle. The pats which were rounded off and tapered stood on the smallest top print.

During my grandmother's time all milk was scalded in pans after the pans had stood in a bath of cold water then placed on a boiler manufactured for the purpose. These boilers were made to take two or more pans at a time, and after having reached a given temperature the pans of milk were taken from the hot water and cooled. The cream is the film or skin which forms and settles on the top of the scalded milk after the milk has cooled. This film or skin was skimmed off to be placed in cups and sold as the famous Cornish Clotted Cream or bulked and made into butter. The scalded, skimmed or separated milk can be used for human consumption, fed to young calves or mixed with barley meal to produce a well-balanced pig food. Householders can quite easily produce their own scalded cream from the full-cream bottled milk delivered to their doorstep. During my grandmother's lifetime, my mother's lifetime and the first part of my lifetime cows were all milked by hand and a fast milker would milk eight cows an hour. When twenty cows were milked twice a day this amounted to five hours of busy work for one man. In addition to the milking, there is the separating of milk, washing every part of the machine, re-assembling, washing the buckets, feeding the skimmed milk to the calves and pigs, taking the cows to the field, and bringing them in at next milking time.

With cowmen's wages now running at thirty five pounds an eight hour day, the labour costs of milking one cow by hand twice a day is over two hundred pounds per week. This is before the cost and housing the animal. Also the maintenance of buildings must be taken into consideration. One man now milks between one hundred and one hundred and fifty cows twice a day with modern milking machines, the milk passing straight from the cow into bulk tanks, having being weighed and cooled to be collected by bulk tankers for transportation to strategically placed milk factories which, over the years, have developed into a prodigious co-operative success.

Several sows were kept on the farm at Trewashford. Their progeny were taken on to slaughter weights as porkers or at heavier weights for bacon. They were killed and dressed on the farm, a few every week, delivered direct to butcher's shops. Mother cleaned the entrails and the maw of the pigs after which they were boiled and sold as 'natlings' or tripe. The large intestines were cleaned then filled with groats or finely minced pig meat to be sold as groat or meat puddings for which there was always a ready sale. It is just not possible to obtain puddings with the special herby flavour that mother made with freshly ground sage from the farm garden.

CHAPTER 3

Learning to take the Knocks

1918 – 1925

In the natural course of events, where there is life there will inevitably be death. My father had built up a very fine herd of South Devon cattle at Trevollard and later, at Trewashford.

Unfortunately abortion struck this herd during 1921 after which there was scarcely a calf born alive for three years, which almost destroyed the herd. Usually the sensible thing to do in these circumstances is to retain the aborted cows in the herd and to calve them again in hope that the same animals would build up a natural immunity to the disease. This works in most cases, but apparently did not in this case. One reason being that too many of these cows failed to conceive after they had aborted. I can well remember the vet arriving to remove retained placentas from some of these aborted cows. It was the cows which had the placenta removed which did not conceive again. At the time I wondered if the infertility of these cows was caused by physical injury to the cow's ovaries when they were cleaned or whether the Lysol, a strong disinfectant, which the vets used to wash the cows out might have damaged the cows' ovaries causing sterilization. Whatever the cause it appeared to happen to the best bred cows. This was a great financial blow as we lost an elite herd of cattle and consequently ran up a large bill for vet's services, a potentially bulk of milk was lost, and also the lost calves which had to be replaced. After the disease had run its course father purchased newly-calved cows to build up the dairy herd. Two out of every three of these purchased newly-calved cows contracted, 'Red Water' one of which would recover and one of which would die. Father was therefore compelled to stop buying newly-calved cows.

Cattle reared on the farm will develop a natural resistance and a natural immunity to 'Red Water' disease which is transmitted by ticks. It was only adult cattle that were purchased which were most vulnerable to the disease. Rightly or wrongly we have always been under the impression that pus from poll evil, emanating from a bruise on the poll of a horse's head which had festered, or the pus from the fistula, a bruise on the withers of a horse, which had festered and exuded pus, contains the same germ which causes abortion in cattle.

We also ensured that horses contracting these diseases did not come into contact with pregnant cows. An eradication scheme which has been conducted during the last few years by the Ministry has almost eradicated contagious abortion from the British Isles.

Not long after the First World War had come to an end, my father had the misfortune to lose five horses over the period of a couple of years or so. One was a young mare called Violet, which father drove to Plymouth in a spring wagon every Friday morning loaded with produce grown on the farm in the form of butter, eggs, chickens, pigs, flowers and vegetables in season. Violet contracted influenza and died. Bedford, an ageing white horse, was found dead in Little Meadow. Prince, another older white horse, disappeared up to its neck in a bog situated between Lower Trewashford and Higher Trewashford. There was not the equipment around then to dig out Bedford and it was impossible to extricate the poor thing alive. Polly, a pregnant mare was found dead with her head resting in a stream between Lower Trewashford and Keason. A year or two earlier Polly had kicked and broken the leg of a smart pony that father drove in a jingle.

Father had gone to Castlewich sale and bought a mare called Maggie which lost her first two foals. He also bought two ex-army horses. One a Canadian-bred horse called Tommy turned out alright, but as soon as the other horse felt the pressure of the collar it would stand upright in the air and fall backwards onto its back. She was unworkable. During the early 1920's a two year old shire filly was bitten by a rabid dog and it died later from the deadly disease. She was one of five horses which died from rabies during the West Country epidemic. This filly had been grazing in a field known as Long Butters which extended in length from Lower Trewashford to the end of the row at Pillaton village. She had become lame, whereupon father brought her to the stable in the farmyard at Higher Trewashford for treatment. On examination, father discovered a wound on the filly's fetlock which he bathed and dressed frequently. Many times I had stood by the side of the filly watching him. I might even have held the filly by its head while father attended to the horse.

One morning after we had left home for Callington School the filly became rabid. She kicked the door of her stable down and escaped to the yard onto the highway. She then galloped in the direction of Callington with father, Jim, and others in pursuit. They headed her off on Amy Down then drove her back to Trewashford Farm where she died. I imagine the authorities came to put her down.

The stark realistion of the dangerous situation to himself and his family caused my father to faint, which is a very uncommon occurrence in our family. It must have been a severe shock to suddenly realise he had been treating a case of rabies with his bare hands. Nothing of what happened on that day was ever discussed or referred to by our parents, Jim or Alma. This information came later from outside sources. That rabies invasion of the South West corner of England lasted for about three years. Messrs John Fursman, Stan, Betty, William Lansley and others were sent to Paris for special treatment after having been in close contact with animals which had suffered from rabies. After these facts were known to us we wondered why our father had not also been ordered to take this special treatment. During the rabies scare my father had arranged for several friends and neighbours to spend a day rabbiting at Trewashford one Thursday in winter. When rabies had first hit the West Country, a law had come into operation which required all dogs to be muzzled when not feeding. Among the party were Bill and Jerry Crago, teenage farmers' sons from Newhouse Farm. William Mutton and his son Sid from St Dominic, Herbert Reap and his son, Louis from St Dominic with Sid Perkins.

These all carried guns, they had also brought spaniel dogs. There were other parties with ferrets, nets and dogs. Father had his dog 'Rose'. Police Constable Warren, stationed at Callington had occasion to visit Mr Martin at Torr Farm during the day. On hearing guns being fired at Torr Farm, P.C. Warren directed his footsteps across the country in the direction of the shooting which happened to have been the stipulated half a mile from any public highway. He came upon father kneeling and listening at the foot of a hedge for the ferret which had not been seen for a while. His dog 'Rose' was sitting unmuzzled by his side while the dog's muzzle was buckled to a button-hole of father's waistcoat. While P.C. Warren was booking father for owning an unmuzzled dog, for which he was later fined at Callington Magistrate's Court, signals were dispatched to the remaining owners of dogs and those carrying guns without licences. Bill and Jerry probably possessed no gun or dog licence, for they collected their ferret, guns and spaniel and made a hasty retreat for home, travelling in the opposite direction to avoid the Police Officer. They were not seen again that day. Sid Mutton and Louis Reep hid their guns, muzzled their spaniels, and set up nets. The other owners of dogs muzzled them before P.C. Warren could visit them. His presence, at the very least, commanded the attention of these law-breakers. Sid and Louis were 'crack' shots. Sid, the last survivor of that rabbiting party, passed on during May of last year eighty nine years old.

After the loss of the mare Violet, father drove the Canadian horse, Tommy, to Plymouth on Fridays for a short while until he purchased a nice looking chestnut horse, with very light feather on its legs called 'Model' for seventy two guineas. When he was young 'Model' was a spirited horse. Father picked up Bert Distin at Burraton on Fridays while father delivered the produce. We were required to bring 'Model' into the stable on Sunday evenings during the summer months because otherwise, he would be getting onto the road to chase the courting couples. It was a strange habit we could not break him of. He developed into a very intelligent horse and was called upon to do a lot of single horse work in the form of hoeing, ridging and shaft work. While reins were always employed he would respond to command and reins were hardly necessary. While still active 'Model' was retired on the farm for about three years until he died a natural death. When Mr Brewer came to collect the carcase I explained what had happened and told him that father had bought 'Model' from a Mr Hatch at Callington Market not long after the war had ended.

Left to right: Sam Keast holding Maggie. I am holding Duchess at St. Budeaux Horse Show, 1923

Mr Brewer remembered 'Model' then. He said, 'I helped Mr Hatch to break him in. He was a bit of a handful and bolted the first time we put him in a wagon. I was on the wagon holding the reins while Mr Hatch had been leading him, and the wagon hit a tree which broke the shafts.' Shire horses with large feet and with heavy feather on their legs are often glamorised by ill-informed, unsuspecting media for their looks. There is no glamour for the horse possessing this skirt of hairs, if their day-long frantic stamping of their feet and the frantic rubbing of their legs against gates or any static object handy are any sign. These shire horses must have always suffered misery and discomfort from the presence and the effects of this heavy feather that folk seem to think so becoming. They are keen and strong workers. Four and a half years ago Trevor, our second son, purchased two filly foals which might, he hoped, in due course, provide his children with ponies to ride. One was palomino in colour (light chestnut with silver main and tail) and one was skewbald, brown and white. Art Cole, from whom Trevor purchased the foals took them back at the age of three years to break them to saddle.

The palomino coloured foal had been sired by a half-linger stallion, a docile and sure-footed breed originated in Scandinavia, which reached a height of around

Chantilly and her foal Montilly by Montasa

fourteen hands. They had been used in their native habitat as beasts of burden in agriculture and forestry.

Art Cole, the owner of the half-linger stallion discovered some moor children actually riding this unbroken stallion around. The palomino coloured pony now known as 'Chantilly' requried little, if any, breaking.

Trevor's eleven and nine year old daughters have ridden her for more than a year as their first pony, so far, without being thrown off.

While the skewbald pony was away at the farm being broken in, she went into a barley field, ate too much barley and died. About eight months after 'Chantilly' returned from being broken in, Trevor said to me, ' "Chantilly" has started showing an udder.' I replied, 'Feed her with a few oats at the same time every day and watch for the kick of a foal.' The presence of a foal was duly confirmed. Art Cole appeared to expect this, for he told Trevor, 'The foal will have been sired by a great grandson of Habitat, the leading Irish sire, a former Derby winner.' 'Chantilly' duly foaled a colt foal. The colt's sire was Montasa, Montasa's sire was Abbott, Abbott's sire was Habitat. One Monday morning, a few months ago, Trevor phoned me and said, 'The colt is unwell. He appears stiff and can only move his eyes. Can you come down?' I answered that it sounded like a case for the vet. He arrived in about twenty minutes. He took one look and gave his verdict, 'Tetanus.

41

Two Shire Foals
It was this shire foal on the left which when fully grown and unbroken to halter was in such pain that it lay flat in the field and permitted me to cut away the frog of its foot which exuded much pus

This is the first case I have seen since leaving college. There is less than one per cent chance of a complete recovery after spending two hundred pounds on drugs. As there is practically no alternative the kindest thing to do is to put the colt down.' Fortunately the children were at school and knew nothing of the sad news until later on in the day, when we could explain to them properly. While we knew horses were prone to Lockjaw, it never dawned on any of us to subject the colt to a course of anti-tetanus injections. Somewhere around 1935, we moved two full-grown, raw, unbroken, shire colts from the Kilquite side of Molenick to a field near Cutmere by road, a distance of about half a mile. Sometime later one of these colts went lame in a front foot and within a short space of time this colt lay flat in the field as if in considerable pain. I advanced very slowly towards the colt, I quietly examined its foot. Its frog was hot, so I took from my pocket a lamb-foot pocket knife and started paring the hoof around the foot where a shoe would normally rest. After a while I found a tiny hole in the form of a black spot in the front of the hoof where a small particle of grit had penetrated. I followed the black spot by paring the hoof until I came to the pus. I went in search of a better knife but failed to find one. I should have used a farrier's bent knife. I returned, sat on the ground, took the colt's foot in my lap and commenced paring. Eventually I pared away the whole area of frog in the colt's foot exposing the whole area where the pus had formed, while the colt lay flat in the field keeping perfectly still.

I phoned Mr Thwaite, a veterinary surgeon, practising from Liskeard. I requested him to come to inject my colt against Tetanus. On arrival he examined the animal's foot and said, 'Who cut away the colt's frog?' I replied, 'I did.' He assured me that I had done a good job.

Soon after father moved to Trewashford he erected two galvanised iron coverings to protect ricks built in the mowhay. The coverings were rigid, each covered a wider, larger corn rick than was normal. Two large poles, equal in size to the present day electricity poles were raised at each end of the rick cover to which a windlass was attached, which raised or lowered the galvanised iron covering with a wire rope. These coverings were not common although I believe one or two had been erected at Keason Farm. At Trewashford, as at most farms of any size there existed a horse round. This consisted of a fixed metal cylinder with usually two poles protruding, one on either side, to which one or two horses were harnessed and attached to walk in a circle. At the bottom of the cylinder were cogs which drove a long, horizontal, metal shaft which entered the barn to drive a reedcomber a chaffcutter, a linseed cake crusher, a threshing machine or a corn bruiser. I have kept horses moving while they have been attached to the horse round at Trewashford while father and the staff made reed, bound the reed in liners and the liners into wads. The reed was used to thatch hay ricks. During the First World War what became known as the 'Corn Law' came into being. I don't know how it worked, presumably it provided a guaranteed price for the corn that was produced. However the 'Corn Law' worked, it was repealed around 1921 and while it lasted it must have produced some cash for the farmers. In fact, it was a year when farming had become prosperous, for, during 1921 my father and many neighbours purchased paraffin vaporizing oil-driven water cooled, stationary engines usually a seven Lister-Blackstone with two fly wheels which required pre-heating with a blow lamp to start it up. This was to replace the horse round.

Mills and bruisers were also purchased to go with the new engine. My father was able to buy a corn sheaf self-binder during this affluent period. The next year, in the month of May 1922 by father bought a left-hand drive Ford T ton lorry to take the farm produce to market instead of by horse drawn vehicle. Hedley, then fifteen and a half years drove this lorry to Plymouth quite often, and, usually twice a week to Callington and Saltash cattle markets without any hindrance by the authorities as to his age. Keason Farm must have installed its stationary engine a few years before 1921 because I remember having seen a large fire at Keason viewed from Hilly Sladeland field at Trewashford one Saturday afternoon which destroyed ricks of straw, hay and possibly one or two windlass operated rick coverings. I heard that the fire had started when the barn pulley shaft resting in a hole in the barn wall against which a straw rick had been built, become overheated catching the straw rick on fire. A second fire occurred in this same mowhay some years later caused, it was claimed, by some youths carelessly throwing away a lighted cigarette end.

Hay harvesting is a strenuous business even today, but when the grass was cut by scythe and later by the horse-drawn grass mower it really was hectic when time would not stand still when the summer sun shone. My father insisted the hay was all turned in the field by hand fork and then stacked by hand fork. The two horse hay sweep replaced the hay wagon, the modern horse rake replaced the 'Tumblejack', my father would not buy either a hay turner or a hay pole to stack the hay. During the early 1920's the single horse wood hay sweep came onto the market to supersede the two-horse hay sweep. I worked the single horse sweep from a boy onward while Hedley who was older and stronger than I, pitched the hay at the rick.

Between 1919 and 1925 the rick was usually made by Jimmy West. The hay was usually pooked in the field to conserve especially during showery or 'catchy' weather. My father was becoming too crippled to pitch hay at the rick himself so he invariably worked the horse from a seat fixed to the rake. My first experience of Callington Council School was an attempt to 'duck me' by the senior boys of the school. As soon as I entered the boys' cloakroom on the first day I was grabbed, but the 'ducking' did not succeed because my hands and feet flew in every direction.

Cordelia soon joined Hedley, May and myself at the Launceston Road Council School where Mr Arthur Bishop, the headmaster was assisted by Miss Owen, Miss Osborne, Miss Rickard and Miss Gwen Bishop. The number attending the school at that time was around two hundred and twenty. There were six classrooms, five of which were occupied which meant, on average, forty four pupils represented one class under one teacher. From what I was led to believe, Mr Arthur Bishop possessed no teaching qualifications as such. He, nevertheless, achieved a very high success rate with those of his pupils who sat the elementary school scholarship examination, the eleven plus, which enabled successful pupils to obtain free education at the grammar school situated in Saltash Road, Callington. Unsuccessful pupils could attend the grammar school by paying a fee for the privilege. I do not recall Hedley having taken this examination and assume my parents paid for his attendance at the grammar school. Had he sat and passed this elementary scholarship examination it most certainly would have been a major surprise to his teachers and family.

He was born on 24th October 1906 in this case his examination would have been taken around 1917 during the First World War. Every spare moment of this period was taken up assisting our father on the 173 acres of farmland. He carried out all the chores without adult assistance. There was no spare time for him to do homework. However brainy he might have been he had no hope of passing.

In every family some child will naturally shine brighter than the others. My sister May was our brain child and it had been expected she would come near the top of the County in this examination. As it turned out she took this examination wrapped in blankets having been quite ill with influenza. Both May and Cordelia passed the elementary school scholarship. I was unquestionably the least clever member of the family. No one even considered the possibility of paying for a grammar school education for me. As I was never a bookworm I gathered from practical experience, observation and trial and error. This proved as good as any other learning for I have never wanted for worldly goods. A. J. Freeman, the Head Master of the Grammar School remarked to Hedley one day, 'So your brother is not considered clever enough to join you at this school.' Hedley was a good farmer, and we remained 'buddies' until the end of his days. But, considering all things I haven't done so badly myself and wouldn't have the events of my life any other way. Not long after I arrived at the Council school a boy sitting next to me pinched a very painful blackhead formed at my stern end, while still in class. I let out such a yell that it was heard all over the school, this brought Mr Bishop to the classroom enquiring of the commotion and what had happened. At morning assembly after prayers had been said and, sometimes after a hymn had been sung, Mr Bishop would read the latest War News from the Daily Paper. I remember him once explaining to us that there was a great deal printed in the papers that was not suitable for children. Those wonderful days of innocence.

Being an ignorant country child at the time many years passed before I fully realised the full significance of this remark. At eleven a.m. on November 11th 1918 pupils were assembled at the school's flagstaff where we sang the National Anthem as the Union Jack was unfurled and raised. After this we were all dismissed for the day.

As the weeks rolled by the only important thing that happened was catching an occasional wild rabbit on our way to school, and letting it loose in the classroom until one day when I gave Ken − a good boy's punch up in the playground for saying something or other about which I regarded as untrue. Ken's mother kept a shop at the bottom of Church Street which Mr Bishop and I passed each day on our way to our respective mid- day meals. Ken had arrived from school before me for, by the time I had reached his mother's shop, she was at the door shaking her fist at me and informing me that she intended to tell Mr Bishop that I had been hitting Kenny. Sure enough, as soon as the school had assembled for the afternoon session Mr Bishop summoned me to the cloakroom. 'Mrs— has been complaining to me that you have been hitting her Kenny.' 'I have, Sir.' 'What was it about?' asked Mr Bishop. 'For spreading untruths about me, Sir.' 'Well now, to appease Mrs— I suggest that you apologise to Kenny. Shake hands and make up.' said Mr Bishop. 'I cannot apologise. He got no more than he deserved,' I explained. 'Come now, Tucker. I think that you should apologise to Kenny,' said Mr Bishop. 'Sorry, Sir.' I muttered. 'Won't you reconsider this?' asked the Head Master. 'No, Sir,' again I emphasised. 'Then, I'm afraid I am left with no other choice than to cane you' said the irate master. 'Then I'm afraid you won't do that, Sir.' I replied.

Mr Bishop returned to his desk to fetch the cane. On his return, he said firmly, 'Hold out your hand, Tucker.' Nothing happened. He repeated the order. Again nothing happened. Eventually he raised the cane above his head as if to strike. That was the signal for me to sail into him with fists flying. We had a rare 'set to'. I have no recollection of the cane connecting with any part of my body. It might well have done, but even if it had, it would have been of no consequence for I had formed my own rules of conduct. No one was going to intimidate John Tucker.

When the 'scrap' had 'petered' out we returned to the classroom to an oral examination. I became aware, and was impressed, that Mr Bishop showed not the slightest malice or ill favour towards me during that examination. He treated me as fairly, possibly more so, than the others. I did receive the cane on a later occasion, but only once. The five teachers took turns to remain at the school during the dinner break. On the November day near the 5th it happened to be the turn of Miss Jenkin who was young, petite and attractive. As she was having her meal in the spare classroom I could, of course, do nothing better than to borrow a 'kicker' firework from another schoolboy, light it and throw it through the open window of the spare classroom where Miss Jenkin sat alone. Had it have been one of the other teachers I probably would not have bothered.

After the school had re-assembled Mr Bishop summoned me to the cloakroom again 'Tucker, did you throw a firework into the classroom where Miss Jenkins was taking her dinner?' 'Yes, Sir.' 'Then I will have to cane you. Hold out your hand.' Whack. 'Now the other.' I held out each hand in turn. No resentment against taking the cane was felt or displayed at receiving this over rated so called corporal punishment, which I knew was fully justified. While at the time I knew it was a foolish thing to do, it is in the nature of most humans, at some time in their lives, to do stupid things. It did, at least, give Mr Bishop the satisfaction of knowing that I could take medicine as well as prescribe it. I fail to understand the rage displayed by a certain section of the community who rail against moderate and reasonable corporal punishment for young offenders provided always that the recipient is actually guilty of the offence of which he is accused of committing. It should be a natural process of growing up to learn to take punishment for doing what is known to be wrong. It should also be acknowledged that to take the 'knocks' of life is also part of that growing up process while one is still young. One is far more able to absorb and to withstand the larger 'knocks' which inevitably evolve in later life. Contrary to what we are often led to believe there is nothing free in this world of ours. Everything, whether good or evil, has to be paid for by someone. So why should not each individual be required to pay or to be paid according to each individual circumstance? Whether there is anyone sufficiently clean, pure and wise to administer justice is another matter.

Boys of the school had regularly played Cowboys and Indians which, as one would expect, could become something of a 'rough and tumble game'.

If one is not prepared to take the knocks, one should not play, and as the Americans say, 'If you cannot stand the heat. Stay out of the kitchen.'

Claude, one of the biggest boys in school, who later became a foreign missionary, brought his father with him to school one day loudly protesting. He came to the school playground during a school break following his father. The father pushed his way through the main concentration of schoolboys, pointing in my direction. As he approached me still pointing, I turned around to seek the object of his concern. He stopped when he came near and said, 'You have been hitting my Claude with a stick.' 'Isn't your Claude big enough to hit back?' I asked him. Claude's father said, 'I'm going to report you to Mr Bishop.' Which he did. I was not summoned to the cloakroom by Mr Bishop on this occasion. Instead, the playing of Cowboys and Indians was banned from the whole school. It would have been a waste of time running to my father for sympathy when I was on the receiving end. This is a case of learning to take the blows both mentally and physically which is natural and necessary in preparation for the hard, harsh conditions one meets in the outside world.

On another occasion the Head Master said to me, 'Tucker have you and Brian Smith been fighting?' 'Yes, Sir.' Brian has complained to me that you had a stone in your hand when you hit him,' said Mr Bishop. 'I did not have a stone in my hand when I hit him, Sir. I most certainly did not.' 'That will do, Tucker. You may go.' As I walked away I heard him say. 'Hold out your hand, Brian Smith.'

It was in the month of March. A Monday, May and I set off in the morning to walk from Trewashford to Callington School. We reached the lane which led to Keason Farm about half a mile from home, when suddenly the sky became dark, it changed from heavy blue to blue-black. An oppressive gloom settled over the lanes. I said to May, 'I'm going home.' She bravely said, 'I'm going on to school.' Before I put my head inside the homestead the cloud burst. Everywhere was soaked with the rain, which came down like stair-rods. All the moveable farm utensils were swimming. A river ran down the length of Hilly Sladeland Field having entered the gateway at the top of the field from the Higher Kernick Quarry area.

Our shearling ewes had lambed a high percentage of twins that year. Twenty seven twins born from these shearlings were in a small field known as 'Gunners Nose' situated near the farmhouse, and many of these very delicate lambs were drowned. Hedley and I spent the morning trying to revive those not too wet by the hearth fire, then trying to reunite the almost unrecognisable lambs with their disdraught mothers. A frustrating and disheartening job. Before May reached school she was drenched to the skin and hadn't a dry thread on her body. Pupils in these circumstances dried themselves out around the coke stove burning in the boiler room under the school kitchens. I have never seen storm rain like that before or ever want to again.

Saving hay at St. Ive Cross in the eighteen nineties
Mr Richard Barrett on pony with four sons. On rick: Alfred Barrett, Richard Barrett, William Barrett.
Standing at the side of the rick: Thomas Barrett and youngest sister Elizabeth Barrett

Soon after morning assembly on the first school day of every month for a couple of years before I left school, Mr Bishop would summon me to his desk, hand me a cheque and say, 'Walk casually to Barclays Bank in the town and cash this cheque for me.' These cheques were usually made out for between ninety two and ninety three pounds and each cheque represented the salaries of the school's five teachers for a month. During each term Mr Bishop visited the other four classrooms in turn for a few days each to examine and to assess the progress of its pupils. During these exams he would set work for his own class and put me in charge to keep them in order while he was away, with strict instructions to report anything amiss which I did not hesitate to do when necessary.

On my last day at school Mr Bishop called me to his desk and said, 'It has not been the custom of this school to present prizes to its pupils when leaving. The school's staff and I have, nevertheless, decided to make an exception in your case. We would wish you to accept these three books together with our very best wishes for your future.' I thanked him most sincerely. Inside the cover of these three books was written: Callington School. Presented to JNo. E. Tucker. For excellent conduct and excellent work. A. Bishop. November 1922. Callington CI. School. Presented

Left to right: Miss Gwen Bishop, Miss Owen, Mr Arthur Bishop, Miss Bessie Rickard, Mrs Osborne, 1918
School teachers Launceston Road Council School, Callington

to JNo. Tucker. A. Bishop . March 1923. Callington CI School. Presented to JNo. E. Tucker. A. Bishop. July 1923. For excellent conduct and excellent work.

One of these book prizes was from a series of 1V Piers Ploughman Histories. Priced at one and sixpence. One was a specimen book on countryside rambles by W. S. Furneaux while the other was a book on geography. The cover of the latter has become detached and lost completely during one of the five house changes since 1923.

Having regard to such a wayward start to one of the most important stages of a human's life in the form of a child's education, the presentation of these three books, however inexpensive, was regarded by me as amongst the highest awards a child could expect to receive whatever the degree of intelligence that child might have inherited. A healthy respect for each other had evidently developed between Mr Bishop, his staff and myself for this unique presentation to have been made.

Over the years I have made enquiries from pupils who attended the school under Mr Bishop's Head Mastership even after I left the school but found no evidence to suggest that Mr Bishop had ever recognised any other pupil in this way.

I had naturally felt slightly inferior at not being sufficiently intelligent to warrant a grammar school education when my brother was considered to have been so, and my two sisters had also qualified in their own right to attend the better school.

This awareness of inferiority instilled a desire, an ambition and determination in me to succeed in the business world and to achieve equality with my brothers and sisters.

Ronald Johns, a second cousin of mine from my mother's side became a teacher at the school before I left. I believe he spent his whole teaching career at that school which has since been extended and, at a guess, it now caters for nearly one thousand pupils.

At about the time I left school Mr Bishop started up a Sunday afternoon Bible class in the West End Methodist Chapel to accommodate the teenage fraternity. The Bible class developed or progressed into what later became known as the Callington Brotherhood, which up to the present time has attracted a large following. It could well be said that Mr Bishop was the founder of the Callington Brotherhood.

Electricity replaced gas lighting for Callington town somewhere around 1920. Rural houses were lit by candles and by single and double wick oil-burning lamps and single wick oil-burning lanterns.

The Aladdin mantle oil lamps and the Tilley pressure oil lamps and lanterns arrived soon after the First World War.

The cleaning of the lamps, the lanterns and their glasses, the trimming of the wicks and topping up of oil was a daily chore.

Crystal wireless receiving sets arrived in Callington soon after electricity. We obtained our first battery wireless sets during 1927. Batteries were charged at Criffle Mill by Mr Harry Harris powered by a water wheel. We obtained our first television set during the 1960's. Our first electric light at Venn Farm was produced by wind power stored in batteries which was installed about 1949. It was about two years later that we obtained light and power from the mains. I left school at the age of fourteen years and two months during July 1923. I had previously worked on the farm from a very young boy doing any work that my immature frame could accomplish without receiving or expecting to receive any reward financial or verbal in addition to my food, which was excellent, my clothes, which were adequate, but usually old fashioned and sleeping accommodation which was very comfortable. I cannot remember my father giving me as much as a copper as spending money or as much as a verbal 'thank you' during my whole life. As children none of us received pocket money to spend as we wished either while at school or after leaving school. The first thing I did when I left school was to buy a new peddle cycle for eleven pounds. The money I had saved over the years from the sale of mole skins and from cash gifts I had received from relatives. At that period children were held responsible for the welfare of their parents. The needs of parents always came first. There was no welfare state as we now know it which took care of the old, young or infirm. There was, of course, the Poor Law Institution known as the Workhouse who took care of the poor folk with no relatives to take them in.

These Institutions were run by Boards of Guardians and my Uncle John Tucker was a member of the local Board. Some cases were extremely pitiful. In the farming sphere the survival of the parents was the primary objective in the hope that at some time in the future children could follow in their parent's footsteps. It was thus that it came about that we, in common with two thirds of farmers' children, left school to commence working on our father's farm without receiving or expecting to receive a weekly wage, and without seeking or expecting an immediate cash reward in addition to board and lodgings.

On leaving school during July 1923, I was sent away for a couple of week's holiday first to Stokely Barton, Stokenham, Kingsbridge with my father's brother, Thomas, his wife Kate and their three children Winifred, John and Edward. Then to Ranscombe Farm, Sherford with my mother's sister Mabel, her husband Cyril, and their three children Herbert, Iris and Arthur. My father arrived at Ranscombe for a few day's holiday towards the end of my stay. While father was at Ranscombe, Uncle Cyril kept saying to him, 'William, I would like for you to look over Venn Farm a little way up the road which is being auctioned in a couple of week's time.' On each of these occasions I heard my father tell Uncle Cyril that he was not interested in looking over Venn Farm. However, before father and I had left Ranscombe Farm for home, Uncle Cyril had harnessed his pony to the jingle and had contrived under some pretext or other to drive father to Venn Farm. Some days later, after having returned home, father took mother to view Venn Farm. And so it came about that on the day that Venn Farm was auctioned at Kingsbridge, my parents attended the sale to purchase the 175 acre farm.

We children were only vaguely aware of what was happening at the time as our parents were not accustomed to acquainting their children with their business affairs. We learned from outside our home what our parents were supposed to have paid for the farm.

Not long after our parents had purchased the 175 acre Venn Farm my father's landlord, the owner of Trewashford Farm, Mr Thurston Collins was found one morning dead under his bed. Mr Thurston's two sons had been killed in action during the First World War. The two daughters who survived disposed of the whole of the estate by public auction during 1924. The estate, which consisted of tenanted farms and dwellings was sold in lots precisely as it had been let which presented an opportunity for farm tenants and house tenants to purchase their dwellings. The auction of the Newton Ferrer's Estate had come as a complete surprise to all of the tenants including my father.

Had my father not bought Venn Farm the year before he would have been in a position to purchase Trewashford Farm, but as he had already committed himself he was unable to back out. As it was he must leave Trewashford Farm and the people he had known for the whole of his life to move fifty miles away to live among strangers. He had made a major blunder and he knew it. A Mr Ned Bond, the grandfather of the present owners of St Mellion Gold Course purchased Higher Trewashford Farm with 114 acres of land for £4,050 for occupation by his son Jack. Mr Harold Martin purchased Lower Trewashford Farm and fifty one acres of land for one thousand and one hundred pounds. The same farm is now on sale for £125,000. Mr Frank Pearce purchased the eight acre field 'Long Butters'. Mr Ned Bond required Higher Trewashford with its one hundred and fourteen acres to be vacated by Michaelmas 1925.

Mr Harry Trant the tenant of Venn Farm was quite willing to vacate the farm to permit my father to enter and occupy it at Michaelmas 1925 had my father so wished. Meanwhile a Mr Cyril Tucker of two hundred and twenty eight acres Molenick Farm, Tideford had decided to relinquish the tenancy of Molenick Farm which was owned by Lord Eliot of Port Eliot Estate, St Germans with a view to farming in South Africa. Instead of moving to Venn Farm my father tendered a rent for Molenick Farm and was granted the tenancy which was to commence at Michaelmas 1925. Mr Cyril Tucker duly arrived in South Africa where a couple of years later he was found dead having been apparently murdered. A Dutchman was later convicted for his murder.

Two fields distant from Trewashford Farm on the top road stood Higher Kernick Cottage with a garden and two acres of land.

The cottages, the garden and the two acre field were owned by the Newton Ferrers Estate and left to Mr Ned Fowell whose two sons, Bill and Edwin and daughter, Jessie lived with him. He had been a carpenter by trade and had met with a serious accident which had left him crippled while engaged in building the Royal Naval Dockyard extension at Devonport.

The dredged sand for the extension works was taken from Start Bay just off the South Devon coast, a short distance from, and almost in view of, where I now sit. The dredged sand left a large hole in the sea bed of the bay. This hole was refilled with sand drawn from around the seaside village of Hallsands by successive storms. This left the village unprotected and at the mercy of the storms until 1917 when an extra severe storm washed twenty seven of the village's twenty eight houses away. A Miss Prettyjohn lived in the house which had been left standing and she remained living in this house for many years after we came to live here in 1944.

Before Ned Fowell retired he worked on the Newton Ferrers Estate travelling to and from his work in a horse and trap.

One night when returning from a Pillaton pub the male staff employed at Newton Ferrers big house pushed Ned's trap onto Amy Down and hid it among the tall furze bushes where it remained for quite a while. When Ned retired from work my father applied for a pension on his behalf and after considerable haggling Ned was granted a pension of one shilling per week which had to be collected from St Mellion Post Office. A distance of more than two miles.

Ned had been a tall man as were his three children, Bill, Edwin and Jessie, all tall and physically commanding people. Bill had worked locally, Edwin had served his time in the Royal Navy and Jessie cleaned the village school and the church. Every Monday morning Jessie also helped my mother with the family wash, where she scrubbed industriously in the massive wooden tub with scrubbing brush, afterwards boiling them in the copper boiler in the washhouse.

One washing day, I entered the wash room where Jessie was scrubbing the clothes. She started talking about her school-girl daughter and Louis. With casual mischief intent I impertinently asked, 'However did it happen Jessie?' She replied, 'Well, boy. It happened like this: I rinned (ran) and Lou rinned, I valled (fell) and Lou valled. My legs flew abroad and Lou flew between them. And thats how 'twas, boy.' I realised that Jessie had scored a monumental six from what can only be described as a very loose delivery. When Jessie cleaned the school and the church, she carried a bunch of large keys on a ring sufficient in size for her to place her hand through in order to carry them. On her way home from cleaning the school one evening Jessie met a local character by the name of George Morrall who was reputed to have possessed an outsize 'limb' with which he obtained free drinks by wiping eight half crowns in line off the counter at Hollands Inn, Botusfleming, near Saltash.

On this particular evening George who casually met Jessie, asked her if he might walk her the rest of the way home. Without the slightest warning Jessie raised her keys and struck poor George with such force that she knocked him out cold. One Monday after mother had left the washhouse to prepare the midday meal, Jimmy West teased her for being so chicken-hearted and cruel in knocking the chap out for such an innocent request. Jessie said, 'Well it was not only that, his name sounded too much like an old cat for my liking. I can't stand cats.' At around nine o'clock one week-day morning during February 1925 I collected a flat poll cabbage to take to a ewe with her two lambs grazing in Mushton Cottage Field which father had farmed since Ned sold his horse and relinquished the tenancy of the field. As I approached the cottage, I saw Jessie standing in the doorway holding a stout, forked hazel stick. Then Jessie stepped forward yelling, 'You are the very one I am waiting for,' at the same time raising the hazel stick and bringing it down in the direction of my head. Instinct took a hand, I raised the cabbage I had been carrying above my head and 'ducked'. The cabbage caught the full force of the blow and shattered into pieces. I threw what was left of the cabbage at Jessie, and beat a hasty retreat with the full wrath of Jessie following me. She threatened she would murder me in the most barbarous of ways. I hadn't the faintest idea what this attack was about. She had said, 'I know you were there because I heard them call you John,' but I had no idea where 'there' was. I returned to the farmhouse to share my experience with my folks whereupon, Hedley burst out laughing. It eventually transpired that, after I had returned home from chapel the previous evening, Hedley and brothers Harry and

Hedley Cloke, the Dolley boys, with some of the other village children when strolling past the cottage had opened the top hatch door and filled the porch with faggot wood stored close by. This made Jessie and her family prisoners in their own home until someone came along and removed the faggot wood. The cottage had been made of cob, its windows too small for them to squeeze through, and there was only one entrance. No wonder Jessie was mad! She never again came to do the washing for us.

The afore mentioned Holland Inn near Hatt, Botusfleming stands along by the roadside about a couple of miles from Saltash on the Callington Road. For a period of each side of 1920 it was frequented by three interesting characters: Jack Anstis, Fred Wenmouth and the afore mentioned George Morrall. Jack and Fred lived and slept in farm outbuildings. I knew Fred better than the others, having conversed with him on many subjects. He was a short, gentle man with a white, flowing beard. He was always clean and spoke in a quiet voice. He claimed that he was heir to one of the landed estates in East Cornwall. Across the road and one field from Holland Inn stands a farm and some high farm buildings. The farm was occupied at the beginning of the century by James Pawley and his wife Mariah. Standing talking in the roadway one quiet, still, moonlit night after turning out time were the 'regulars' from the Inn, who clearly heard the voice of Mariah calling to James from upstairs, 'There be a circle around the moon, James.' James voice, also loud and clear, probably for the benefit of the listeners exclaimed, 'Aye, an' there be a circle around ther' ol' ass Mariar.'

At the turn of the century, a wild fowler by the name of Jack Anstis, who might have been the same man who called at Holland Inn, baited mallard with apple pips and cores obtained from local cider presses at selected places along the banks of the River Tamar. Early mornings with his duck gun loaded with pellets mounted on a punt, he would drift within range on the tide to blast the feeding mallard. He had been known to kill seventy birds with one blast.

Frank Welch, who once lived in Lockyer Cottage, knew a lady who also lived in Lockyer Terrace. This lady kept a dog and a cat which at night slept in the kitchen. On returning to the kitchen one morning this lady found the cat sitting on a chair washing itself, all that remained of the dog was its four paws. She had paid forty pounds for the dog which was a chihuahua.

While on the subject of dogs, almost all farmhouses possess two stairways, one of which is near the front door and another sometimes near the hearth. A Cornish farmer owned a terrier dog which slept in an armchair situated by the stairway door and near the open hearth. The dog had watched its master lay the firewood on the hearth so many times, that when one morning the farmer overslept the dog decided that it was about time it started laying the firewood in place itself.

When the farmer eventually opened the stairway door he was more than a little surprised to see the terrier carrying the firewood to the hearth. The farmer encouraged the dog until it became quite adept at laying the firewood every morning before the farmer entered the kitchen. This went on for some time until one morning when the farmer overslept again. This time when the farmer entered the kitchen the terrier had laid the fire in the hearth, it had pulled a chair to the fireplace and was actually standing on its hind legs on the chair attempting to reach the matches, which were kept on the hearth mantel shelf.

CHAPTER 4

From Depression to Second World War
1925 – 1939

When May attended Callington School she practised playing the piano and she played the organ at Pillaton Chapel from the age of nine years. She also took her turn playing the pipe organ at Tideford Wesleyan Methodist Chapel and is currently playing the organ at Dobwalls Methodist Chapel when required.

Cordelia has played the organ at St Germans Chapel for many years.

Our father would take us children to the eleven a.m. Sunday Methodist service at Pillaton while our mother stayed at home to prepare a roast dinner for the family and also for the preacher of the day. During Sunday afternoons we were packed off to Sunday school when Mr Nun Barrett took the entire class. Mr Barrett was a naturally serious man, I cannot ever remembering seeing him smile. While he read and proclaimed the scriptures with clarity he did not always command the full attention of his class for I seem to recollect that he frequently admonished his class in the following manner. 'It is hard that we cannot come here to sit quietly and to pay full attention for what, after all, is only a very short time, to the reading and to the studying of the scriptures.' This he repeated weekly, in the same low unemotional bass voice. Our mother attended the evening service with us children as we became old enough to attend.

The preachers who came to stay with us came from all walks of life. They included the Methodist minister, the member, or prospective member of Parliament, solicitors, business men, tradesmen, farmers, butchers, bakers and candlestick makers, some sincere, some not so sincere, some radiating the joys of life, some serious.

I have seen preachers tie hessian sacks over their boots to enable them to walk long distances home on ice-bound roads after taking services at Pillaton Chapel during the hard winter of 1916. I have often wondered why they bothered to leave their own warm homes. There was dear old Billy Jane from Dunnerdake. On Saturday afternoons his wife would take over his job, whether it was ploughing, or muck spreading to send Billy into the house to prepare for the following day's preaching appointment, for which he was usually late. His excuse was either that a cow had unexpectedly calved 'a booteful heifer calf' or a sow had farrowed 'ten booteful veeres'. Mr Jane drove a horse and trap to his preaching appointments. For much of the distance between Pillaton Chapel and Dunnerdake the road was covered with high trees, and pitch dark when there was no moon. The River Lynher runs perilously close to the road in places. Mr Jane told us that when driving home in the dark from his previous appointment at Pillaton, he had gone to sleep, and he only awoke when one wheel of his trap crashed down from a high bank. On one occasion Billy was preaching about the River Jordan, hugging the Bible, Billy fairly shouted, 'Now dear friends, the River Jordan was a mighty river, not one of these yer little ol' piddlin' streams that you often see around here.' Then there was Hallelujah Buckingham from Callington, a burly coach-builder with a strong voice. His favourite text was 'I am the vine, Ye are the branches'. Then there was Billy Dingle from Bowling Green, Callington, the grandfather of the Foot Family who kept a few cattle for a hobby. While inspecting his cattle early one Sunday morning prior to fulfilling a preaching appointment Billy saw a man apparently working in an allotment field. This man in the allotment field also saw Billy Dingle. Wishing to avoid Mr Dingle the man took evasive action but Billy, who had been riding a horse, soon cut the man off.

When Billy had finished admonishing the man for being in his allotment on a Sunday, the man turned to him and said 'It is alright for you to talk Mr Dingle. You have been at home most of the week to do as you wish, while I have been away at work from dawn to dusk, all the week. I cannot accept that there is any more harm in me collecting food for my family on a Sunday morning than there is in you worshipping your cattle on a Sunday morning.'

In complete contrast was the Reverend Tommy Buttle of the United Methodist faith stationed at Callington. His favourite story was the Chest of Drawers which he had made out of his own head with enough timber left to make another. Tommy was a true Christian. This fact caused real embarrassment to his wife and to his family, Eva, Ida and Thomas Arnold as he would frequently arrive home minus one or more of his garments which he had presented to someone he had met who had been in greater need than himself. This impulsive generous gesture kept the family quite poor. Thomas was a school mate and friend of mine. My sisters May and Cordelia lodged with the mother of Thomas Arnold for a while when we moved to Molenick at Michaelmas 1925. The Reverend Tommy Buttle had laboured in the poorer parts of London during his ministry and he knew at first hand what poverty meant. Where in the year 1993 can you find another Tommy Buttle?

I possessed a lively, very enquiring mind and I began to question the power of prayer during and after the carnage which took place during the 1914–18 War. I have continued until the present day to question the power of prayer. Is prayer anything more than a time-consuming ritual? Is prayer anything more than someone expecting another to make dreams come true when they could be attempting to make this same ending complete themselves. Is prayer anything more than an excuse for laziness? If Tommy Buttle prayed he also fulfilled that prayer to the limit of his ability. If we are absolutely truthful we are bound to accept and to admit that prayers cannot possibly be answered from the outside. Prayers can only be answered from within our own selves. Let the beauty of Jesus be seen in me. Not until we all stop playing God, not until we all accept the facts of nature and the facts of life, not until we all replace greed with compassion will the Gospel of Jesus and the Gospel of Martin Luther King bear fruit. As a child I was taught by theologians that God created and placed man on this earth with a free will to do as he pleased. I took this to mean that God would not be answering prayers. So, I stopped praying and have not prayed since. I have relied on my own judgement as to what is right and what is wrong. I have done right as far as my will power will permit. I have to answer only to my own deeds, therefore am not afraid to meet my maker. If others must pray, then they must.

With few exceptions, organised religion has been used to exploit and degrade man's less talented and less fortunate white-skinned, black-skinned and coloured brethren. White Bishops live in pomp and splendour in their palaces built by slaves, while the followers of the Bishops worship their stone idols in the form of massive cathedrals not caring about the pain and industry suffered by the workmen who built them. Thousands upon thousands of hungry, less fortunate human souls every night sleep in discomfort on park benches or in damp, draughty, cold alleyways. What a reflection this is on those people who presume to call themselves Christians – followers of Jesus. Prayer has not created comfort or a full belly for these less fortunate sufferers. Compassion is not enough. Praying did not stop the First World War. Praying did not stop the Second World War. Praying has not stopped the Irish from quarrelling and killing each other. Prayer has not stopped the squabbling and the killing among humans around the world every day. Praying has not, as yet, filled the bellies of the 40,000 human souls that die every day from starvation and the lack of pure water to drink in various parts of the world.

Death from starvation can be caused by civil turmoil, strife between nations, by money spent on guns instead of food, by drought, pestilence such as, locust plague in Africa, the inability of nations to balance the human population with its available resources of the necessities of life, transferable wealth, by mental ability to plan or an unwillingness among the nation's wealthy subjects to share.

If praying could induce the wealthy subjects within a nation to provide food to keep the world's annual 14,600,000 deaths (from starvation alive) would this be anything more than a stopgap solution which could backfire by producing still more humans to feed? If humans are unable or unwilling to control their own destiny Nature will control it for them.

Jesus gave, Tommy Buttle gave, but organised religions exploit and take.

Hymn singing has drawn more people to Christian places of worship than has reading the scriptures. Over the centuries gifted people have set beautiful religious phrases to equally beautiful melodies which have provided immense pleasure to as many humans in the past, and doubtless will continue to provide immense pleasure to humans for as long as humans and human sentiment survives, even when beautiful phrases have not been born of logic. No one has enjoyed singing these beautiful phrases taken from the scriptures more than me yet when I do join in singing 'All things bright and beautiful, All creatures great and small, All things wise and wonderful, The Lord God made them all', I have to admit to myself that all things are not bright and beautiful to all creatures.

Many things are sordid and very cruel. Neither are all things wise and wonderful to countless humans and living creatures on this earth, certainly not to the 40,000 humans who die every day from starvation, and natural disasters and certainly not to the thousands of animal victims who fall prey to animal predators. Having lived so close to nature I am unable to accept the claim that a caring compassionate Creator created living creatures which depended for their survival by cruelly devouring defenceless members of other animal species. Having lived with these country ways for so long and having observed Nature's ways I am therefore unable to accept that a caring compassionate Creator would set up a jungle sphere where only the strongest survived and where the weakest always went to the wall. This is the complete opposite of what Jesus taught when He was on earth. Do we believe the story of Jesus or do we believe the story of the Creator God? Or are we really so naive that we believe both stories?

The Industrial Revolution which came to this country during the latter part of the nineteenth century was followed by decline in industry at the beginning of the twentieth century when other industrial nations, notably Germany, commenced manufacturing their own goods. The employment of subsidies and tariffs together with the manipulation of the money market also restricted free trade between nations. This hastened the decline of British industry which directly affected the income of the working man. That led to the growth of socialist organisations and to strengthening of trade unions which drew up their rules in such a way as to further reduce competitiveness with other nations. The Parliament of 1918 was elected by almost complete suffrage with men over twenty one and women having the vote at thirty. By the end of the 1914–18 War British trade had further declined as developing nations no longer wished to import our manufactured goods, and because of this home producers were unable to sell our goods at cost price. To make goods more competitive, employers reduced wages and increased working hours while the government handed back the coal mines to their owners who had received subsidies while the emergency lasted. A railway strike took place in 1919 and a coal strike in 1921. The workers including women who had performed the jobs of some men during the war and the former servicemen returning from the war, had been expecting prosperity from the peace, and not unnaturally, became angry when this didn't happen, and the dismay felt led to the miner's and then the General Strike of 1926.

The 1926 strike failed after a few weeks because strike breakers volunteered to keep the wheels of industry going, to stop what many considered a revolutionary step by the trade unions. Although the miner's strike continued it eventually ended in much bitterness. The recession became worse with a return to the Gold Standard at a rate which made British goods uncompetitive with those made abroad. Farmers suffered severely from 1920 onwards when the prices of farm produce fell sharply. Many farmers were bankrupted including men who had returned from the war to start off at high prices often on borrowed money, and many only survived by unpaid family labour. After the First World War the U.S.A. provided substantial financial support in the form of loans to the Germans which enabled them to make reparations with American dollars. Production exceeded demand and down came the U.S.A. economy with a crash. This in turn brought about Protectionism culminating in the Ottawa Agreement when preference was given to trading with Commonwealth countries. Improvements in trading with Europe began around 1934–35 by which time a Second World War was predicted and European countries began preparing for the time when war might again bring starvation and despair for millions as it had done in the previous war.

It was not until the end of the 1939–45 War that land values increased, when agricultural prosperity with inflation made farming one of the most advanced and productive industries in the country but the tragedy for Britain was that it took a war, with all the traumas of battle to restore agriculture to its proper place. Are there any lessons that we can learn in 1993 from the past events with regard to industry and labour relations?

The financial depression, of course, soon affected us. I heard Mr John Roberts who farmed at Landulph by fattening bought-in store cattle, say at the end of 1923 that the cattle that he had bought in the spring of 1923 and sold during the autumn of 1923 had realised far less money than he had paid for them, after having spent more than seven hundred pounds on purchased cereals for cattle food. The depression accelerated as the years passed until the collapse of Wall Street during 1929, when many people who had suffered financial losses, some their entire life's savings overnight, had jumped from high buildings, or had expressed the disaster in other dramatic ways.

As the depression accelerated it became increasingly evident that my father had tendered too high a rent for Molenick Farm to be able to survive. Fortunately the Government had abolished Land Tax somewhere around 1927 or 1928. While this had eased the financial situation slightly it still remained desperate. My father then applied to Lord Eliot through Mr Gordon Brenton his estate agent, for a rent reduction. The amount of reduction could not be agreed between my father and Mr Brenton, but the agent did consent for the rent to be fixed by independent land arbiters. It came about that Messrs John Pearce of Plymton Land Agents and Valuers were appointed rent arbiters for Molenick Farm. Mr John Pearce and his son Mr Frank Pearce duly arrived at the farm to set the rent. They valued separately ostensibly to test the ability of the, then, young Mr Frank, to value to the satisfaction of his father. The decision of each proved almost identical, the result being that my father's rent was reduced by five-eighths, to three eighths of what he had been previously paying. This was a reflection of the state of farming at the time. Two other tenants of the estate had also been granted permission for their rents to be fixed by the independent land arbiters at about the same time as my father. After these results became known the estate refused permission for their tenants' future rents to be fixed by arbiters.

The financial recession continued into the 1930's. To their credit, the Port Eliot Estate voluntarily reduced the rents of all the farm tenants on the estate, on a temporary basis. While some of the estate's tenants were still unable to survive the financial recession, my father just managed to do so, possibly for the reason that my mother, and us children worked long hours for him without demanding financial reward in addition to the board and lodgings. When my father moved to Molenick Farm at Michaelmas 1925 he engaged the services of two workers who had previously worked on the farm for Mr Cyril Tucker (no relation). One was a Mr William Symons having sixteen years experience and he gave us also, sixteen years good service after which he retired. The other was Mr William Hill who had worked on the farm since leaving school, he lived on the other farm at a Kilquite during 1928, he left Kilquite to farm for his father, who had now retired at Pensilva Farm.

Early in 1929, at the age of twenty two years my brother Hedley, married Daisy, and they moved into Kilquite House where there were some buildings suitable for housing cattle and a few pigs. It had been the custom when a farmer's son weds a farmer's daughter for the bride or the bride's parents to furnish the house and for the groom or the groom's parents to furnish the farm with live and dead farming stock. While Hedley had married a farmer's daughter my mother had purchased some second hand furniture to set up the newly weds. There was no money available to set Hedley up in a farm so he then worked on the farm to receive the 'going' wage of thirty two shillings per week. Hedley and his wife commenced keeping a few chickens, pigs and I drove the Ford one ton lorry which he had driven since the age of fifteen and a half years. When father and I went to market we also took the vegetable produce which Hedley and Daisy had produced from his two acres and sold it to the shops. Hedley was paid every penny the produce realised. During 1939 he was accepted as a tenant of Cornwall County Council smallholding of around fifty acres near Kilquite known as Tilland Road Farm. Apart from being given a few sheep by his father he had progressed entirely from his own and his wife's efforts. During 1937, he tendered for the 64 acres Tredudwell Farm owned by Messrs Betty Brothers and was accepted. He purchased Tredudwell Farm a few years later.

During this period, and until 1940 my father was paying interest on a mortgage on Venn Farm which was substantially more than my father was receiving in rent from the tenant of Venn Farm, although at the time Hedley, May and I were not aware of this. Several times after I reached the age of twenty years I had asked my father for a little spending money to enable me to maintain my status with my boy and girl friends. Every time I asked, my father told me that he could not afford to allow me any spending money. Since I was twenty years of age I had driven the Ford ton lorry, I handled what was at the time a fairly large amount of cash each week obtained from the proceeds of sales of farm produce delivered and sold to Plymouth and Devon shopkeepers, every penny of which I had placed on the kitchen table on my return.

During the early summer of 1931 when I had reached the age of twenty two years, I entered the kitchen just before one o'clock one Saturday for my mid-day meal, as was usual, to see the wages of William Symons lying on the end of the long kitchen table awaiting collection. My father was seated at the end of the long table, apparently reading the daily newspaper, which was held up in front of his face. Looking at the money on the table and also at my father apparently intent on reading his paper, I asked, 'Dad, could you spare a ten shilling note for me, please?'

My father uttered not a word. Possibly for the reason that he had not replied, I said, 'Dad, I will take the ten shilling note that is left for Symons.' I took the ten shilling note and placed it in the inside pocket of the coat I was wearing. My mother had heard and seen what had happened and she replaced the note with another. Neither my father nor my mother had uttered a word. As my father had been holding the paper up in front of his face, I had been under the impression that he had not seen where the note had been put.

The mid-day meal proceeded as normally. As it was a Saturday, I should have taken a couple of hours off for a break before milking time and feeding the animals but I had never taken advantage of this. Instead, as soon as the meal was over, I picked up a shovel and a digger and proceeded along the drive across the orchard to the cattle yard to rebuild a stone hedge which the cattle had torn down. On entering the cattle yard I had taken off my coat and hung it on the gate which was some little distance from where I was working. After working on this stone hedge for some little time I thought I heard a sound coming from the direction of the gate where my coat was hanging. I stepped backward from the stone hedge sufficiently far enough for me to observe my father taking the ten shilling note from the inside pocket of my coat. With the shovel in my hands, I watched while my father recovered his ten shilling note, after which he proceeded slowly with the aid of two walking sticks across the orchard and out of sight, moving each foot only a few inches at a time. My father had not spoken at all and neither had I spoken during the whole time. I stayed leaning on the shovel for a long time and felt really sorry for myself. At the age of twenty two my prospects were really depressing. I knew that if I threw my hand in, my prospects might have been even more bleak for without my free labour my parents would have been compelled to sell up while the price of everything was on the floor. I knew that I was trapped. I also knew that if I held on there was always a chance that conditions would improve even if the chance appeared mighty slim. I also felt very sorry for my father. His financial situation must have been really desperate to force him to deprive his own son of a measly ten shilling note that he had rightly earned. The situation would not be improved by angry exchanges. For the whole time I had worked on his farm I had put the welfare of him, his livestock and his crops before my own welfare. While I had done my share of grumbling I had never shirked work or stopped working besides that, I had never threatened to stop working. No son could have been more loyal to his parents. It had been an unusual situation for in spite of being denied my financial rights I had been one of the happiest, if not actually the happiest person in the Parish, quite possibly the happiest lad in the County. I was always singing, possibly because I possessed nothing. I hadn't a care in the world. I returned soberly to my task of rebuilding the stone hedge that afternoon completely without malice, hoping that one day I would be repaid for my services to my parents.

They were very religious, so religious that only special papers were allowed to be viewed and read on Sundays.

We were never permitted to play cards at home. Our father once, after we were grown up, found us playing cards with our cousin Iris Haddy in the lower kitchen, he took the cards and threw them on the fire. While during his latter years I often shaved him on a Sunday, something he never did himself on a Sunday.

My faith in my parent's religion suffered most that despairing Saturday. 'Like as a father pityeth his children so the Lord pityeth them that fear him', had been a frequent text by pious Christians.

Why should anyone 'fear' anyone? My father may have needed pity. God also may have needed pity, I most certainly did not. I had no reason to 'fear' my father or God. My father had no reason to 'fear' me. I respected him and was entitled to his respect. I was a grown man. I was entitled to have been told the reasons why my father could not pay me wages. This knowledge would have made a very painful episode more bearable. If my father's respect for me was a reflection of God's respect for me, it speaks little for God's respect for me. It's the law of the jungle all over again.

My father had been aware that he had made an outsize blunder when he purchased Venn Farm and moved to Molenick Farm. Apparently he could not bring himself to discuss the affair with his children which caused a barrier of uncertainty and mistrust. Apart from a weak chest, a legacy from pneumonia, I was healthy and strong and I felt quite surely that I was entitled to some recognition in return for my loyalty and dedication. It would have been to father's advantage financially had he confided in us.

Left to right: Louis, May and Rodney

I had attended Sunday school at Pillaton also at Tideford Methodist Church on Sunday afternoons, which were presided over by seventy year old, legless Mr John Drown who drove a pony and trap, also moved around on a hand-propelled tricycle and two small boxes. I carried him in and out of Church with an arm around him many a time. Tuberculosis had made it necessary for the amputation of his legs when he was a young man.

Whenever possible we permitted our employees to take Sundays off, which made extra work for the family. It meant changing from Sunday clothes to working clothes several times. It also meant travelling a mile or two each way in all weathers often on foot. During my lifetime I have heard many comments how lucky I had been to have been born a farmer's son, including some disgruntled employees, some of whom complained that their sons would lack the opportunity to become farmers as have my sons. Maybe I was lucky, maybe our sons are also lucky, but the luck might not in fact have been as glamorous as it appeared had all the details been known.

May married Louis on the second day of June 1934, when May was twenty two years of age. May, like Hedley and myself had worked long hours seven days a week, for fifty two weeks in the year since leaving school for no cash payment apart from food, clothes and lodgings. One year while Hedley was living at Kilquite Farm House he was too unwell to work during the corn harvest and during that time May pitched all the sheaves of corn grown on forty eight acres with a fork, from the wagons to me on the rick and as the rick grew bigger, the work became harder. May married a farmer's son who was six years her senior, he too had worked for his father under the same conditions, workwise, as we had done. May's father-in-law gave Louis three in-calf cows for his services when Louis married. When the first of these cows calved, his father asked for the cow to be returned. His father actually sold the newly-calved cow at Saltash market. When Louis and his three brothers had finished work at eight p.m. one Saturday evening, after having spent the whole week in the hay fields, their father took them into the garden and said to them, 'Now then boys, off with your coats and stick in here for an hour.' When May married Louis all she took with her for her seven year's work on the farm and house was the clothes she possessed, plus her 'war savings' contributed during the war years while attending school, which amounted to thirty pounds. With this she purchased a cow and a dining room suite. May's wedding dress was paid for by withdrawing dividends which had accumulated from the Saltash Cooperative Society. May told me that soon after she married I gave her enough money to purchase a cow, which amounted to fifteen pounds. I have no recollection whatsoever of doing this. I have no idea now where the money came from, but from whichever source, it was honestly come by.

Who today would become a farmer's son or daughter under those conditions?

I saw the 'Spirit of St Louis', piloted by Col Charles A Lindberg, pass low directly over Molenick Farm on the evening of his historical solo flight from New York to Paris in 1927. We also followed his progress from commentaries on the wireless, and his reception on arrival at Paris Airport during darkness.

During the early part of one night in the early 1930's we saw the most spectacular Aurora Borealis (Northern Lights) ever seen in the South West of England. It resembled fairyland, high clouds were crossing and re-crossing with the beautiful varied colours constantly revolving and exchanging, it lasted for hours. It was an unforgettable spectacle. Also at some period during the 1930's viewed from Molenick I saw the R100 sister airship to the airship which crashed on its maiden voyage with heavy loss of life, flying over Plymouth.

From the latter half of the First World War onward, the father of Hedley and Harry Cloke owned a pick-up type of motor car with a foldable hood, with the registration number DR100. It was necessary for Mr Cloke to negotiate a blind corner on his exit from Warren House Farm and he habitually climbed from his car to view the road around the corner to make sure the way was clear. He would then rush back to his seat and drive at speed around the corner before any other vehicle had time to reach the bend. This worked for a while until, eventually there was a collision, because another car came along quicker than Mr Cloke expected.

Between the two Great Wars it was a common sight at night to observe many searchlights lighting up the sky and criss-crossing to reach the high clouds. After the First World War there was a dear old couple that I visited on summer evenings who later came to live at Torr Farm with sons, Jack and Heber. These lads, and another son had served in the war, sadly the third son had been killed in action. Every Saturday morning by four thirty Heber had harnessed a horse to the spring wagon loaded with farm produce for his parents to drive to Plymouth Market. One bitterly cold, dry, frosty, February morning his mother had seated herself in the spring wagon, his father was preparing himself to get aboard when Heber said, 'Father do you think it would be any good sowing a few turnip seeds today?' Father said, 'What do you want to sow turnip seed for, Hebe?' 'I thought they might come to market,' said Heber. ''Tis no good they won't grow,' said his father. Whereupon his mother leaned out over the wagon and said to Heber, 'Hebe, if I were you I'd clap 'em een.' Dear old Mr Martin told my father after chapel the following morning, both laughing about the phrase which became a household joke 'clap 'em een'. When Hedley visited Jack and Heber one summer Sunday morning he found them in the hay field. On the Saturday morning, having been short handed, they had decided to sweep the hay with a single horse sweep near to where the rick would be built the following day. Unfortunately it had rained heavily during the night so they were sweeping the hay from around the rick and spreading it around the field again. During January 1935 Mr Harry Trant, the tenant at Venn Farm died. His widow asked my father if he would release her from the farm tenancy at Ladyday 1935 instead of Ladyday 1936. This my father did, possibly unwisely, for it left only a short period of time to find a suitable tenant for the farm. Not only that, had he required Mrs Trant to carry on until Ladyday 1936, it would have given him time and the opportunity to have considered the wisdom of moving to Venn Farm himself, and relinquishing the tenancy of Molenick Farm. He reached the decision on his own without giving his adult family a chance of expressing an opinion and, together, weighing up the pros and cons of this new idea.

Only one man tendered for Venn Farm and he proved to be as poor a farmer as Mr Trant had been a good one.

This was about the time when financial returns from farming were at their lowest. A time when my father had sold a good, fat South Devon heifer at auction for as little as fourteen pounds. When Hedley purchased what proved to be an honest second-calf cow for eleven pounds ten shillings. When the majority of shearling South Devon breeding ewes were sold at Kingsbridge Sheep Fair at between twenty three and twenty five shillings each. When I purchased my first South Devon ram for my father for two and a quarter guineas, the equivalent of forty seven shillings and three pence. This ram had been bred by Mr Sandover of Renton, Kingsbridge and it proved to be one of the finest specimens of the breed we had ever bought. In around 1919 my father had paid thirty two guineas for a ram bred by Mr

Fairweather of Malston farm, Sherford. This sum was, at the time, the breed's highest recorded price for a ram. Six week old farrows were changing hands at between five and eight shillings each. Plate maize could be bought for as little as four pounds and five shillings per ton, as also could French wheat and Russian barley. Potatoes were sold off the farm for three pounds per ton. It was difficult to sell potatoes to merchants at that price if you did not owe them money. For quite a long period of time only William Symons and I worked on the two hundred and twenty eight acre Molenick Farm, except for assistance at planting and harvest time. While William Symons, the horseman, had attended to his working horses on Sunday mornings and Sunday evenings when they were lying in during the winter time, I did the milking, calf rearing, feeding cattle, and sheep at week ends on my own. (During 1938 possibly due to the effects of the Spanish Civil War, the price of wool rose slightly). Some little time later Albert Courts left Tideford School to work on Molenick Farm. Since Hedley had left Kilquite Farm House for Tilland Road Farm, I had been blindly running Molenick Farm organising general maintenance, buying and selling cattle, sheep, seeds, fertilisers, corn, cattle and pig meal, planting and harvesting the crops and selling the produce. As his gammy leg made father a cripple and not much assistance on the farm, most days, when weather permitted, we harnessed the pony to the jingle for father to drive around to his heart's content. It was a ludicrous situation where an unpaid employee ran a business not knowing whether his boss was in a financial position to pay for farm stock and food. In fact, this employer frequently told his employee the goods he ordered might never be paid for. In spite of this I kept buying and selling. It was, undoubtedly, an unusual situation which, surprisingly, went on for years.

A Cornish Farmer's Fate.
A farmer knocked on the Pearly Gate,
His face was scarred and old,
He stood before the man of fate,
for admission to the fold,
'What have you done?' St Peter asked,
'To gain admission here?'
'I've been a farmer, Sir,' he said,
'For many and many a year.'
The Pearly Gates swung open wide
As St Peter pressed the bell.
'Step in and choose your harp,' he said,
'You've had your taste of Hell'.

One day when I was in my early twenties, I was moving a fairly large flock of sheep from Kilquite Farm to Molenick Farm by road. It had been customary to take the sheep across Meladrim Field to cut off a corner. On this occasion there were other sheep in this field which meant that there was no choice but to take the longer route by road, around Meladrim Field. However, taking the sheep round by road meant taking them up a dark, narrow lane called 'Darkie Lane'.

At the time it had been a deep, narrow cutting, although during the last war the Americans widened this lane to permit their vehicles access immediately prior to D-Day. At the time I had a useful dog with me, but try as we did we could not drive this flock of sheep up the lane, and I thought to myself, 'What a ripe contrary lot.' It was, for some reason, necessary that they should reach Molenick but they were determined not to be driven, so what was the solution?

As a last resort I walked up the lane and I called to the sheep to follow me. Without hesitation, and without further fuss, these sheep followed me up that lane and all the way to Molenick Farm with the sheep dog following behind. 'There', I thought 'I have been taught all my life that a good shepherd will lead his flock rather than to drive them just as I have been doing.' I would not accept what I had been taught, I had to learn from experience. Perhaps I was only capable of learning from experience or was it because I deliberately refused to be taught by others? Whichever it was, I definitely learned that day.

Quite by chance, when I was in my middle twenties, I found myself in the company of a very highly respected Wesleyan Reform Methodist minister by the name of Rev. N. S. Lobb. This minister showed keen interest in farming in general, and sheep in particular. I thought at the time that it might have been because his flock of human souls came from a rural area, mainly with a farming background. I later learned that his son was training to be a farmer.

After recounting some of the management problems which he had encountered among his large human flock, including some of his tupping and lambing problems probably, with the control of his flock uppermost in his mind he said to me, 'Frederick William Faber could not have known much about sheep when he wrote the hymn, "Souls of men, why will ye scatter like a crowd of frightened sheep", could he?' I said 'How do you arrive at that conclusion?' He said, 'If you go into a field where there are sheep with a dog, these sheep will always run together and crowd. They will never scatter.'

I said, 'Yes, I know they will,' but the facts are that it is not natural for sheep to be confined to small enclosed spaces. Sheep by nature are loners. The natural conditions for sheep are wide open spaces where they can see afar, to be driven before the wind over the next hill to the lee of the next hill for shelter, as opposed to cattle who will face the wind, and walk straight into the wind to find shelter. Given sufficient space and natural conditions, each individual sheep will select its own grazing area away from other sheep, and will remain in that area for the remainder of its life if permitted to do so. When the single sheep is confronted with a dog, it will become frightened and will scamper away in the opposite direction to the dog,

69

or to appear to scatter. Frederick William Faber must have been acquainted with hill sheep or sheep used to open spaces.

Being loners, not closely acquainted with other sheep and not thickly stocked, the first reaction of these lonely sheep to anything strange would be to scatter, or scamper away.

That was why the silent type of Border Collie was bred and developed to work quietly, silently, and stealthily in preference to the startling, barking, noisy old English type of Sheep Dog.

For while the silent Border Collie would have little influence when moving a flock of three hundred sheep along our Devon or Cornish lanes, the Border Collies are in their element on the open hills and mountains. It is in the Devon and Cornish lanes that the barking, noisy old English Sheep Dog comes into its own. The Reverend appeared impressed and surprised. Incidentally the true old English Sheep Dog was born without a tail. I believe this was the only type of dog born tail-less. There is no proof to tell us if there still survive dogs who are born tail-less. The current old English Sheep Dog that we see around were born with long tails, which have since been docked. They are importations from America, they are not the true old English Sheep Dogs, they are fakes.

While on the subject of dogs, the following happening might be of interest. The time was the early years of this century, and the story concerns what its owner had considered to have been perfection in animal breeding. It concerned a Mr Eliot who at the time farmed Smeaton Farm in the Parish of Pillaton and his Pointer dog 'Carlo', which had been especially bred to scent the precise position of its game quarry, whether pheasant, partridge, woodcock, hare, rabbit or whatever. When the Pointer dog had determined the exact position of its quarry it would stand motionless on its three legs, one front paw raised, its nose pointing to its quarry, its tail fully extended and it would remain standing in this position until its owner arrived on the scene to 'flush' the bird, hare or rabbit, hopefully to shoot it.

Smeaton Farm is owned by the Duchy of Cornwall, and the game on the Duchy Farms is not retained by the owners, but is included in the tenancy. Mr Eliot was a renowned shooting sportsman and to assist him in this sport he had, over the years, bred many generations of these Pointer dogs before producing this one perfect specimen. During the summer evenings after the day's work had been completed, and after taking tea, it was the custom of Mr Eliot to walk the farm to inspect the cattle and sheep. He also took the opportunity of taking his Pointer dog 'Carlo' with him for the dog's daily exercise. On returning from one of these late evening strolls towards the end of June, he realised that 'Carlo' had not returned home with him. He waited up all night, he retraced his footsteps the following morning. No 'Carlo'. He advertised, he scoured the area. 'Carlo' had vanished completely and he gave up all hope of ever seeing him again. Then at the beginning of August, when cutting a field of wheat with horses and a self reaper, he came across 'Carlo' in the middle of this wheat field, still pointing at the pheasant which it had found a month earlier, having waited all that time for Mr Eliot to come along to 'flush' and shoot at it.

Now you might ask how a dog could live for that length of time without food or drink? Someone did actually ask Mr Eliot this same question but he claimed that his dog possessed sufficient intelligence to attend to the calls of nature during the hours of darkness, to return to its vigil before the break of dawn. That must have been some dog!

From about 1930 until I left Molenick during 1941 I became friendly with a Mr Gimblett who at the time had farmed a County Council Farm adjoining Molenick. With his wife he also sold vegetables, most of them, home-grown from a van and from a shop at Saltash. Mr Gimblett was the father of eleven children (they were not Catholics). He had returned from Canada to join the British Army at the outbreak of the First World War, in which he came back shell-shocked and together with many other shell-shocked soldiers spent some years in a hospital camp at Weard Quay, Saltash. However, he recovered sufficiently to take up farming. We were friends, possibly because I would listen to his war experiences and because I shared his belief that another World War was in the offing. As a race, Germans are industrious and virile. The humility of having her South West African colonies taken from her after the First World War by the Treaty of Versailles and her need, as an industrious nation to expand required only a minimum of intelligence to conclude that the only way for Germany to obtain room for expansion was by force.

Mr Gimblett was reared on an estate at Tregear, and grew up with the son of the squire who was about the same age. They became friends and called each other by Christian names. Between 1930 and 1941 when I left Molenick he had often spoken of Tregear, and of the happy times he had spent with the squire's son. I visited him when he was ninety and I noticed that he never mentioned Tregear. I said to him 'Mr Gimblett, have you ever been back to Tregear to visit your boyhood friend, the squire's son?' He looked at me and his face creased, and the tears rolled down his cheeks. After a while when he had regained his composure, he said to me, 'John, I met him, I held out my hand and said, "Edward". But abruptly he said, "It's Major now"'. 'The tears ran down his cheeks and I realised Time had not stood still for the two old 'buddies'.

Some members of Weard Camp had been provided by the County Council with a house and an acre of land at Blunts to re-establish themselves. The occupants were permitted to do as they pleased with the acre of land, and some put up small sheds to keep a couple of pigs. A cockney Mr Wythe was the possessor of such benefits and he had firstly erected a shed. He asked Mr Gimblett to accompany him to Liskeard Cattle Market one Monday to advise on the purchase of a couple of pigs. Two white slip pigs were duly purchased, and later established in the cockney's shed. About a month later the Cockney invited Mr Gimblett to view the progress of these two pigs.

When Mr Gimblett arrived at the shed, he was surprised to see two black pigs. He said, 'Where are the two white pigs you bought at Liskeard?' The cockney replied 'These are the two white pigs that we bought at Liskeard.' 'Then what have you done to them?' asked Mr Gimblett. 'I have blackleaded them,' said the cockney. 'Whatever for?' said the worried Mr Gimblett. 'Well,' said the cockney, 'after you left me, when we bought them, I heard one farmer say to another that black pigs thrived better than white pigs. The second farmer agreed with this, so I figured it would pay me to blacklead them.' The cockney took on a post round and he began discussing with Mr Creber of Trewandra Farm what he should do with his acre of land. Mr Creber told the cockney that if he decided to plough the acre and to plant it, Mr Creber would lend him a quiet horse and a saracuse plough. In due course the cockney borrowed the plough and Mr Creber's horse. When he returned the horse and plough, Mr Creber asked him how the work went. The cockney replied, 'Very well, but the plough did a lot better job going one way than it did going the other.'

As a townsman he didn't know that the breast of the plough had to be turned, Mr Creber thought, 'We have a ripe one here.' When the cockney asked Mr Creber what he thought was the best crop to plant, Mr Creber told him that bran was selling as well as anything, that bran would always be wanted and that the cockney could plant the bran by hand himself, thus avoiding the need to borrow a horse and drill. He suggested that the man plant bran. So the cockney clapped in bran!

'Lend and lose a friend.' is unfortunately an all too true maxim. It was around 1937 when Leslie, one of my pals, a neighbouring farmer's son, who had been working for his father on the same conditions that we were, decided that, as the best years of his life were passing by without the slightest prospect of any financial reward coming his way, he would take the plunge. So he had taken a job as a travelling salesman for a firm manufacturing veterinary products, which meant calling on farmers. This needed transport and he had no other wheels only his bicycle. He came to me one evening, on his pedal cycle to enquire if it was possible for me to loan him the necessary cash to purchase a motor cycle. I said to him admiring his 'get up and go' attitude, 'I have very little, but whatever I have you can borrow.' I returned from the house with three pounds. I said to him, 'Leslie, that is my entire financial possessions. I am sorry it is not more but if that is of any value to you, you are very welcome to it.' Leslie took the money. I did not speak to Leslie again for more than twenty five years. I had, on a few occasions, seen him at a distance, but he had always contrived to avoid me. I would not have imagined that Leslie's job had been a huge success. He joined the R.A.F. as a mechanic and left the district soon after war had been declared. While in the company of one of his sisters some years later she told me, 'Leslie did buy a motor cycle but no one knew from where the cash came to buy it.' Later on I said to her husband 'I lent Leslie three pounds to help purchase the motor cycle. It would have cost much more than three pounds. Do you know Jim I have not seen Leslie to speak to since the day I obliged him.' Jim explained helpfully that Leslie intended to visit them. 'I will bring him along to see you.' Jim kept his word and brought Leslie, his wife and family. Jim asked me if I had taken advantage of reminding him of that past loan. But I had to tell Jim, 'I could not embarrass him by doing so. I have progressed to the state where three pounds is of little importance.' Nevertheless, I have drilled it into my children that they must not lend to a friend or relative unless they can afford to give the money. Giving is far less likely to cause friction than lending. In which case, if you cannot afford to give, do not lend. Trevor was recently persuaded to attend a bank conference between branch managers and their clients. The theme of all the speeches was that the bank's customers should always regard their branch manager as their friend. Trevor afterwards told them that the advice offered was quite the opposite to his father's teachings. He explained he had been taught quite early in life: If friendship is to last then never borrow or lend. Every business transaction must be entered into on a business footing.

CHAPTER FIVE

Partner and Parent

1930 – 1940

Cordelia married Herbert, a chartered accountant on December 27th 1939 when she was 24 years of age. Herbert had joined the R.A.F. On leaving school Cordelia had worked for Herbert's father, who worked for the Inland Revenue. A year or two later Herbert's father and Cordelia were moved to the Inland Revenue offices at Phoenix Buildings, Princess Square. Plymouth. Cordelia had lodged at home since leaving school. I never knew, asked or was told if Cordelia had subscribed to her board and lodging between the time she left school and the day she married. That was a matter entirely between our parents, but I was aware that she had not done a stroke of work on the farm or in the farmhouse except for herself. There had never been the slightest animosity from any member of the family over this, I merely state a fact. Soon after the outbreak of the Second World War on September 3rd 1939, the Government set up County Agricultural Committees comprising experienced farmers with executive powers to enforce Government policies for food production. This time, food production, was among the nation's priorities in the light of past experience. About the middle of November 1939 my father received instructions from the Cornwall County Agricultural Executive War Committee to plough and to plant a stipulated acreage to cereals and potatoes on Molenick Farm. Not long after he had received these instructions I said to him, 'Dad, the responsibility for this extra planning and extra work will be falling on me. I must surely, by now, have served a sufficiently long apprenticeship to justify being taken into partnership.' Whereupon, surprise, surprise, he raised no objections. So, in due course, we proceeded to the Liskeard branch of Barclays Bank, where father had been banking previously, to sign the necessary document. After the documents to confirm the existence of the partnership had been signed, the branch manager, a Mr LeWarne, put his hand on my shoulder and said, 'Young man, I do hope that you realise the extent of the responsibility which you have just taken on.' This remark shook me a little, I thought I had done just this all along, at least, to others, or did he mean responsibility to my own self? The more I thought about it the more I became concerned. He would have known only a little, if anything, about my character. What had he meant? It was then that I realised that I had not enquired anything about the state of father's business affairs. Were there any outstanding debts? And what was the extent of his assets? It began to dawn on me that I had been absurdly naive taking so much on trust. Was that also the reason for Mr LeWarne's remark? Or was there something else? Had he perhaps doubted my ability? He might justifiably have harboured some doubts. At the age of thirty years I was in my prime. What I did not know, I could soon learn. Apart from this weakness in my chest, I enjoyed good health, I was fit and I was in business, so away with morbid thoughts, let's have a bash!

Notwithstanding, I have often pondered the reason which had prompted Mr LeWarne's remark. We never met again.

Having become a partner in the business, I was entitled to the keys which unlocked the oak, roll-top desk, where my father had kept his business secrets, his cheque books and his bank statements. He had always kept this locked and the keys were always kept on his person. On our return from the bank, I obtained the keys from him, and opened the desk to discover that he had bought Venn Farm for four thousand and six hundred pounds plus three hundred pounds for two substantial, recently built semi-detached houses at Coles Cross, which stood adjacent to the farm. Of the four thousand and nine hundred pounds which father had paid for Venn Farm and the two houses during 1923, he contributed two thousand pounds of his own money, while two thousand and nine hundred was mortgaged, raised from private sources through his solicitors. There were no outstanding debts to anyone from the farming business at Molenick Farm. The mortgage on Venn Farm was the same amount at 1939 at it had been at 1923. The interest on the mortgage on Venn Farm had been greater than the rent received from it. The difference from the mortgage and the rent having been made good from the profits of the farming business at Molenick Farm. In actual fact, the wages to which Hedley, May and I had been entitled had gone to supplement the mortgage interest on Venn Farm. Had we been paid wages, the interest on the mortgage could not have been met. It could perhaps have been said that the finances were not as bad as they might have been. The fact that we had survived was in the circumstances quite an achievement, but how much more satisfactory it would have been had our father discussed his affairs with us children. It was his nature to be secretive, and that was that. While, on occasions, I had grumbled because I had no money to spend like many other working class people, neither I nor any other member of the family ever blamed our father or criticised him for having purchased Venn Farm, resulting in our financial mess. It would have helped enormously had he been able to talk to us. For a problem shared is a problem halved. Hedley often complained to father about working for no financial reward and I heard my father more than once say, 'You can have it all after I'm gone.' He never once answered me in that tone of voice. During the period that we three children were working long hours for such a small reward, my father was paying a substantial sum of money every year to the already bleeding, rich, Anglican

Church Commissioners in tithe levied on Venn Farm. Yes, I accept that my father knew that he would be liable for paying this tithe before and at the time he purchased Venn Farm. We had no reason for complaining. I also discovered that he had contributed five pounds to Dr Barnardo's homes every Christmas for as far back as his records went.

A neighbouring farmer had permitted an employee with a large family to fence off two acres of land for the purpose of keeping a cow to provide milk for his family. This employee duly purchased a cow which died from the effects of Red Water. This employee saved up and purchased another cow which also died. In a book in a drawer of the roll-top desk were the names of a dozen farmers who had contributed to the cost of purchasing a third cow for the unfortunate man. I also discovered that our father had tried to sell Venn Farm several times during the depression, but no one had been interested in buying it at any price. My father was seventy three years of age and almost a complete cripple when we became partners. It was now entirely up to me to put the financial balance sheet right. How much confidence, I wondered, had Mr LeWarne in my doing this. As the war progressed trainloads of children from the cities were distributed around the countryside for their safety. Several arrived at St Germans Railway Station and were dispatched to villages in the area where they were dispersed in private homes. Bill Dave of Cutcrew Farm delivered three children to Molenick Farm for my sixty five year old mother, with a helpless crippled husband, to board and lodge, eleven year old Leslie Scales, fourteen year old John Russell and his seven year old sister Eileen. Bill Dave himself took one eleven year old boy home for his fifty year old wife and daughter to provide for.

John Russell returned to the house one day as proud as Punch, carrying a pheasant which he had clubbed to death when he had discovered the bird sitting on its eggs in one of the fields.

I was working on a machine one evening a short distance from the backdoor of the farmhouse when I saw John Russell chase Leslie Scales into the farmhouse brandishing a fairly large stick. As Leslie entered the farmhouse door, John Russell shouted, 'Come out here, you yellow rat.' Fred Gimblett joined me where I was working and so had John Russell. After Leslie joined us I said to him, 'Leslie, did you hear what John Russell said to you just now?' He answered, 'Yes, John.' I went on, 'Leslie are you going to stand for that?' He said, 'No, John, I'm blowed if I will.' Leslie turned to John Russell and delivered such a perfect left fist on John's chin that he dropped like a tab. After John Russell recovered he turned on Leslie Scales. Leslie was teaching John a lesson. The fight happened too close to the farmhouse which brought father to the door and he ordered both boys to bed. I entered the kitchen soon after the boys and said to mother, 'Don't deprive them of their supper.' I said to Leslie, 'Grin and bear it.' He answered quietly, 'Alright John.' The next day I said to Leslie, 'I've seen John Russell chasing you with a stick a time or two before last evening. You did not attempt to stand up for yourself on any of these occasions. Why?' Leslie said 'Well, John, I wasn't in my own home, was I?'I said, 'That was a very good reason, Leslie.' I did not see John Russell chase John with a stick again.

The war was being waged on Plymouth, and the sound of bombs falling from enemy planes when they blitzed the city upset Leslie. He would often come to my room during the night and say, 'John, there is someone outside my window.' I would go to his room to listen, but, it was either the sound of raindrops falling on the roof below his window, or one of the trees creaking when swaying in the wind. He reached such a nervous state that we put his bed in my room, then he wasn't satisfied until I stood my twelve-bore double-barrelled shotgun in the corner of the bedroom, and put cartridges under my pillow in case the Germans came. This pacified him.

I joined the Home Guard, and about once a week I spent the night with three other Home Guards, on high ground overlooking Tideford. Leslie would not stay at home, he insisted on going on guard with me carrying a fairly large toy gun. Leslie grew up to become a very good cyclist and he often rode in the Round Britain Road Race sponsored by the Milk Marketing Board and also in races abroad. One year he came in second in the Round Britain Milk Road Race. He later became Secretary/ Manager of the British Cycling Club's team and travelled extensively. He had visited us a couple of times since we came to Venn Farm. We then lost track of him until Michael, our eldest son, went into a Kingsbridge cycle shop to buy two cycles for his children, when the proprietor mentioned the name Leslie Scales. Michael told him, 'My father knew a Leslie Scales.' It transpired that Leslie had been 'best man' at the wedding of this Kingsbridge shopkeeper. We later learned that Leslie had come to live in Devon, but sadly before we met again we heard that Leslie had died suddenly from a heart attack. Plymouth suffered many raids from the Germans in this war that could have been avoided, because when Winston Churchill, who had earlier moved from the Liberals to the Conservatives, tried to awaken Britain to the dangers of the Nazi regime the Liberals and the Methodists branded him as a warmonger.

Harry Worth had left school to work at Molenick Farm until his father was recalled for service in the R.N.V.R. when Harry returned to carry on his father's smallholding at East Wall, Tideford Cross. Two bombs fell on one of Harry's fields, but the first did not explode. When the police arrived Granfer Holding, with a dozen children around him was ramming an iron bar down into the fin of the bomb. I was detailed to guard this bomb for a part of the following night, and it was detonated the following day. I had heard this bomb whistle as it fell, the previous night, without exploding. I heard other bombs whistle down without exploding when I was working at Molenick. Many were never found. One evening after dark when the enemy planes commenced their raids I turned the cattle loose from their stalls, just in case. I was leading three horses from the stable when I heard a bomb whistling down quite close. I dropped their halter stems, and dived for the shelter of the low stone wall. There was an almighty explosion, the whole place shook and slates rattled down from the outhouses. It frightened the horses which galloped away. The bomb had fallen into the same field at East Wall, a short distance away, as had the previous unexploded bomb. It left a massive crater.

George Moore and Jim Holding had joined the Molenick Farm staff. This was in stark contrast to the First World War when my father was left on his one hundred and seventy three acre farm without any assistance. In addition to an adequate staff we had also purchased a Standard Fordson tractor and a two-furrow plough.

I was not single at the age of thirty one either from choice or lack of girl friends, but through force of circumstances as my father, a cripple, with a considerable overdraft, relied on my assistance completely.

Also, I had been penniless up until last November 1939. Considering asking a girl to share a home with my parents was unthinkable. When my sister May married, my mother found the extra work a burden, so engaged a young girl called Evelyn Welch who proved to be an amiable, industrious maiden. She turned out to be a superb cook, an expert needlewoman and spotlessly clean and particular in household duties. She fitted into the routine of a busy farmhouse as part of the family. As the years went by we grew to love her quiet, gentle ways. I always admired her hair which was an unusual colour of brownish-auburn. Also she had a deep loving tenderness for all creatures and when the household chores were finished she would set herself to care for the motherless lambs and kittens who responded to the leisurely comfort of her competent fingers.

Nature, being what it is, and the circumstances being what they were it takes very little imagination to foresee the result when I say that Evelyn and I celebrated her twenty first birthday in the most natural of ways. Unfortunately, Evelyn's mother visited my parents when she became aware of the situation even before I knew myself that I was to become a father. Her sparse flatly-pronounced words caused a commotion so great that my mother dismissed Evelyn immediately. Our parents had taken it upon themselves to plan our future before Evelyn and I were permitted to speak. Apparently we did not count. I had learned to take it, but it was going to be disastrous for Evelyn as we had always been in sympathy with each other's thoughts forming an unconscious bond of friendship sharing the 'daily round, the common task' together as pals. No two people could have known and understood each other better, and I challenge the strictest judge to condemn us. Decisions had to be made. I could demand my half share of the business worth nearly five thousand pounds which would have totally shattered my parents, both financially and physically and marry Evelyn or stay on until the end hopefully salvaging their affairs. Whichever the outcome someone would suffer.

A member of the family once asked me why and when I fell in love with my wife.

While I am familiar with, and recognise, sacrificial love including mother-love which exists in all animal species including mankind, I haven't the faintest idea what love is.

Novelists make money abusing the over-worked word of love, viewing it from different angles including the eternal triangle where participants quarrel and fight tooth and nail even unto death. The Anglican and Roman churches issue from their portals the wonders of a special love, but many logically-minded people often ask: 'What does this special love provide apart from entertainment?'

All I know is that Evelyn and I 'soldiered on' amicably, both before we married and after. In truth, we were two of the most tolerant people, devoid of foolish impetuosity and have enjoyed forty four years of contentment, happy in the knowledge of each other's absolute loyalty. Readers may analyse this summary as they wish.

As soon as my mother learned I was to become a father she said, 'We will give notice to quit the farm. We will sell up.' That was all she said, that was all anyone said. No one said to me, 'What would you like to do?' or, 'Would you like to carry on the farm?' I was granted no say in the matter, even after giving freely to them of my best for over seventeen years. I had lowered my mother's moral standards and shattered her moral dream. She had adjudicated, and that was that. I was fully aware that my mother had given her all for the family over the years. Perhaps this was the very last thing that she expected to happen. It would appear that this was the very last thing she had wanted. I had never before heard my mother adjudicate in a business matter for this had always been left to my father. So, when she spoke I had no choice but to treat her decision with the utmost respect, and to resolve my own problems the best way I knew how, without the assistance of anyone. There was little doubt that I had shattered her religious concepts and beliefs. In her eyes I had transgressed and committed the unforgivable. From now on she would require me to stand on my own two feet or to lie on the uncomfortable bed I had made for myself. I had accepted my mother's adjudication without raising the slightest objections, even as I had accepted the humiliation of my father taking the ten shilling note from my pocket nearly ten years earlier. I had long since learned to live with disappointment and learned how to adjust my life to those around me.

I was relieved that I had secured a partnership in the business. I would have been in trouble if I hadn't.

If I was a partner in my father's business I was not a tenant of Molenick Farm, in which case, if my parents decided they were going to give notice to quit that farm there was nothing I could do to stop them. Looking back, the amazing thing about the whole affair was that there was never an angry or cross word uttered against me, or anyone else in this unpleasant business.

Not one angry or cross word has ever passed between any member of Evelyn's family and myself. I accepted the situation philosophically. I had always been happy and singing. I wasn't shattered.

It was, in all probability, the most sensible thing I had done in my whole life. It was as though I was being released from bondage. I had been dominated by force of circumstances and my parent's wishes for the whole of my life. Nothing was likely to change in the current set up. I have never opposed my parents before, I had never been in a financial position to oppose them now. It was a matter of carrying on to exploit the circumstances as these new facts presented themselves. I am afraid I had not shared my mother's unaccommodating religious beliefs in spite of her exemplary example. My observations, my experience of life and of nature in its many and varied aspects, had forced me to question too many of the, then, current religious claims and beliefs and, to question is to doubt. So, regardless of Christian ethics I was left with no other choice but to hold on tightly and grimly to my hard-earned financial connection with the farming business, in the hope that when the farming partnership was finally dissolved I would be in a financial position to throw off my shackles, to start up in my own business, free to do as I pleased. Since November 1939 when I had become a partner in the farming business, I had done little homework. I had figured that, with a little luck, I might hopefully come out of the partnership with just enough money to set myself up in farming at Venn Farm. I was careful to keep my own council over this. Had I been prepared to have been perfectly honest with myself, I would have been forced to admit that I had had a belly full of Molenick Farm. It was not that the farm had been useful, it was an early farm and the land was grateful. It was what was known in the hilly West country as a one-horse farm. The farming drawback in those days was the rabbit population. Many rabbits inhabited the woods which extended the length of the farm. The Estate gamekeepers never bothered to catch the rabbits living in the woods. However well we kept the rabbit population down on the farm it became re-infested with the progeny of these wood rabbits every summer. This created friction between the landlord and tenant from time to time, for it is not possible to farm any land which is overrun with rabbits. I spent much of my time chasing and killing rabbits, this being an unprofitable way of spending time. There were far more advantageous things to do with one's hands. There were no woods which could harbour rabbits near Venn Farm. Since those days (during 1950's) a virus known as myxomatosis was introduced into this country, which killed all but one in ten thousand rabbits. Even so, the rabbit's high reproductive potential ensured their survival. It also ensured massive deaths which were very unpleasant. For the seventeen years since leaving school I had been required to spend too many hours of each day working in order for the family to just survive, therefore my only recreation or sport was confined to catching and killing rabbits. This constant work had almost turned me into an obedient, impersonal machine. It had always been my wish to possess three children of my own. In the main, it was this ambition which had fired and stimulated my devotion to the farming business. The prospect of any wealth without a family to share it had no appeal for me. I could see nothing in life worth working for, apart from a family of my own.

My father had been forty four years of age when I was conceived. It had not taken me long to observe that children born to young parents usually enjoyed a happier relationship with their parents than did children born to ageing parents. At the age of thirty one any man who had worked the hours that I had, who had been as industrious and dedicated to his work, should have been entitled to father a child, if he so wished, without being required to answer to, or be punished by fellow men. I had been in debt to no one. I had long been disenchanted with the interpretation of the Scriptures which my parents and my Christian acquaintances had portrayed, believed and pursued. My personal experience of nature prevented me from accepting the supernatural inferences attributed to creation, the parables of Jesus.

The concept of a supernatural creator having survived a billion, billion years, and more, to survive for evermore is totally beyond me. I am mentally capable of equating to the period of time that I have resided on this planet. I know nothing of its origin or the origin of its inhabitants. I am never likely to learn the origin of this planet Earth or the people thereon, or how or why the sun, the moon or the stars maintain their respective positions in the firmament, or how or why this planet Earth maintains its orbit. It is surely sufficient for one's peace of mind that we keep the Ten Commandments, regardless of whoever created them and regardless of how the world was created, or that we do our level best to keep the Ten Commandments while on this earth, that we follow the example of Jesus while He was on this earth, for no other reason that we do so, not for any reward either on earth or in heaven. Why must we always expect a reward for everything we do? It is deceitful, it is misleading, it is unfair for any society to impose upon or to inflict upon the innocent, trusting, easily influenced, highly vulnerable minds of children, the concept of a supernatural, spiritual sphere from whence we all came and whither we must all go. It is sufficient for their needs that children are taught that, for the sake of their own happiness, for the sake of the happiness of the people around them, and for the sake of the peace of the world, selflessness, tolerance, respect, for their fellow man and a willingness to share their assets, whether mental or material, with those less favoured, is the only logical religious concept at the disposal of the human being. The person who has done nothing for others in this life, has done nothing for themselves. I had neither the time nor the inclination to study modern books. I can only recall reading one book right through my whole life, and that was 'The Children of The New Forest', but I did have the opportunity to study nature and humanity from real life on the farm. Having studied nature so closely I was unable to accept the interpretation attached to nature by the Scriptures as too many religious theories and religious teachings had contradicted obvious facts, while nature for its part was also frequently at odds with religion and its teachings.

I have observed the actual conception of a thousand domesticated animals each year of farming. I had personally observed the births of many and the deaths of many more. I concluded that had not the conceptions that took place every year not taken place at that precise time, not one of these specific conceptions would ever have taken place at any other time. Any other second of time, and some other spirit would have been conceived.

Humans multiply in precisely the same manner as do animals, which strongly suggests that no human life was predestined. If, for example, a human female produces twelve reproductive eggs a year for thirty years, this is a potential three hundred and sixty children. When one, or two, or three or more of these eggs are fertilised, she will normally produce three or more children. Should any one of these eggs divide in its early stage, it could produce as many children as there are divisions. While each reproductive egg within a human is a potential child, or children, each is distinct from another. Each and every human, whether conceived inside or outside of wedlock has one opportunity and only one, to be conceived. If that opportunity to be conceived is lost it is lost for ever. As also happens with every species of plant just one living seed from many living seeds in every species will be germinated to survive, to see the light of day. One potato tuber from twenty or more will be planted every year to produce the required amount of potatoes. One grain of maize, wheat, barley, oats or rye out of every forty or fifty grains from each species will be planted each year to produce the required amount of cereals. It is the same with the fertilised common domesticated hen egg, many of which are consumed as food, fried, boiled, poached or scrambled or beaten up for baking, or eaten raw by magpies, jays rooks or crows. It is only the very few lucky eggs, or the very few unlucky eggs (depending on the prevailing circumstances) which are incubated, hatched and reared.

Every human, animal, or bird that is on this earth, has arrived here by chance. Many will also leave the earth by chance. As with the incubated hen's eggs, as with humans conceived, or with animals conceived, for some it will become a happy event, but for many it will be disaster. Life is an immense lottery. For the forty thousand children around the world who, we are told, die from starvation every day, for the countless numbers of children who are aborted, the lovely touching story of the guardian angel watching over each one of them, must be, to them, a monstrous unmitigated myth, a fallacy and an insult. The many religions, with their varied ideals, with the implications of their ideals, well meaning and sincere as they sometimes appear, are unable to withstand the logic of the realities of life, or of nature. Those beautiful words which so many of us treasure and love to sing, 'All things bright and beautiful, All creatures great and small, All things wise and wonderful, The Lord God made them all' must have sounded highly immoral and a mockery in the ears of the starving or the aborted child. The beautiful words of the Twenty Third Psalm and the equally harmonious melodies which have been set to the Twenty Third Psalm and the many touching hymns and melodious, sentimental, and religious songs will also sound tuneless and sad to a starving or ill-treated innocent child. Are we all morons?

We have been told that this psalm and hymn singing did fall on deaf ears and sounded a mockery to some young British lads floundering in the mud, in the blood of their comrades, and in the bitter Arctic weather conditions of the Flanders trenches during the First World War, while they were waiting to be wastefully sacrificed as cannon and machine-gun fodder by the thousand and tens of thousands, to satisfy the whims of incompetent generals and politicians who deceitfully claimed that God was on our side, for this is what we were taught at Pillaton School at the time.

The delightfully worded and harmonious hymns and psalms must have sounded weak and meaningless to the many victims of the civilian bombings on both sides of the battle line during the Second World War, to the Jews in the German concentration camps, to the millions of Russians who died, to the Poles, Hungarians, Vietnamese, Afghanistan, to the displaced peoples of the world, to the mariners who were torpedoed and left to the mercy of the cruel sea during the two World Wars, to the victims of the natural disasters and tragedies that plague the world, or to the countless numbers of defenceless animals, large and small, who are hourly brutally sacrificed as food by and for the survival of animal predators including the human. It is anything but a beautiful experience for victims of animal predators.

It might have been observed that the forty thousand humans that die every day from starvation belong to those races which lack the mental ability to generate their own species at a rate commensurate with the amount of food available for the race's full survival. The poorer the race, the faster will the race multiply. The more affluent the race the slower that race will multiply. The poorer the individuals within a race, the faster will these individuals multiply when they meet and mate with poor individuals. This appears as a natural process. This would appear to be beyond the influence of a possible God, but not beyond the influence of the Roman Catholic Church whose creed is to multiply regardless, faster than any other religious sect, so that in time through sheer numbers Roman Catholics will command the power to dominate and to rule the earth. In my view the concept of any organised religion of whatever creed is to rule mankind on earth, using fear and mysticism to attain this objective.

It is worth noting that in a civilised society it is usually the children who are imposed upon, exploited and treated inconsiderately who will remain most loyal to their parents rather than the children who have been idolized, petted, pampered and lavished with the good things of life and provided with all the things they have coveted. Parents will receive far less loyalty and devotion from children they have petted, pampered and lavished with their wealth. Nine out of ten foals reared by hand, which have been pampered and petted, will acquire vices which will prevent them from being trained for useful work. As with pampered children, these pampered foals will reach the state where they are only fit for the knacker's yard. There is a natural tendency for pampered children, foals, workers, and for pampered employers to become selfish.

Having become disenchanted with the religion of my parents as it was presented to me at the time, I had decided that, for the sake of my own future and the future of my family, my own personal financial wellbeing must from now on take precedence over all else, regardless of the more popular orthodox religious and moral ethics.

It had appeared to me that throughout the centuries the various religions had created and formulated their own forms of religious and moral ethics to suit their own financial needs. The time had arrived when I must form my own religious and moral ethics to suit my own financial needs. I had been my family's puppet for long enough, for not only had my parents been supported by my industry and dedication, the survival of the farming business would eventually also benefit other members of the family. Under the circumstances, could I relinquish my financial partnership in the farming business, which was my passport to freedom? This left few practical options open to me. I could not leave the farm, or my mother, with father in his condition, an able-bodied man was needed on this farm at all times. The independent streak in me would not permit me to condescend to ask to bring a wife into my parents' home, since they had made their views so abundantly clear. I had once asked for ten shillings wages a week, this had been refused. I would not risk being refused a second time.

This, then, was the ultimate unforgivable disgrace, which it had generally been considered I had brought to the family name, and on my family's religion.

As time passed some of my senior relations, and several of my pious acquaintances, would have murdered me with their looks, had their sharp glances been capable of killing me, and had I permitted them. When they attempted these tactics, I always held their gaze firmly until their will gave way. I never needed to wear coloured spectacles to cover my embarrassment as do normal wearers of dark glasses. I could look anyone straight in the eye without in any way feeling uncomfortable. I carried on living as normal, possibly brazenly. A few derogatory remarks against my actions or inaction, as the case may fit, filtered to my ears by diverse ways. This was normal, and in the circumstances acceptable. I took my mother to Callington for some, now forgotten, reason, where we ran against Fred Ryder who, when newly-wed during 1904, had occupied Torr Farmhouse for six months to fulfil the terms of my father's tenancy agreement when my parents moved to Trevollard. He said to my mother, 'I have just heard about your terrible business, this unfortunately is what happens after one has done their best for their children. I am sorry for you all.' I walked slowly on while they stopped to talk. I must confess, I did show a bit of a grin. It was probably a wry, grim grin, but it was, nevertheless, a grin. Fred had ignored my presence. Had a stranger been listening to that conversation they could have been forgiven for concluding that my parents had been keeping me. In fact, I had been earning my keep from an early age. I had always put my father's livestock and crops before my own personal interests. I remember once, one summer's day on a Saturday about mid-day when I was in my mid twenties, a young man of my acquaintance arrived on the farm in his car with two young ladies. They begged me to join them to make up a foursome to partner an attractive daughter of a successful business owner for an afternoon by the seaside. I declined the invitation because I was needed at home to supervise the harvesting of a field of hay. No one could have been more loyal to their parents even though I was unpaid. That was life. It was significant that not one person possessed the courage, or had attained the peak of perfection necessary to approach me personally on the subject, which fact itself spoke volumes. I, likewise never excused, or ever attempted to excuse, my actions to anyone. One of my pleasures of life had been singing at my work, I was told that, I had been heard singing about mid-night while milking the cows by hand, after helping Hedley with his harvesting until very late at night at Tilland Road Farm, without payment or thanks from anyone. In spite of, or perhaps because of, the current situation, I continued as before singing at my work.

The situation did not depress me in the slightest. On the contrary, for the first time in my life I had good reason for singing, and a very good reason for working. I possessed something worthwhile, something tangible to live for. As my entire wealth was tied to the farming partnership, I would not be free to do as I pleased until the partnership had been dissolved. So, when the time came, when my parents produced the necessary twelve month's notice to vacate Molenick Farm at Michaelmas 1941, I delivered the notice to quit for them by hand to the Estate Agent at the Estate Office at St Germans, on the morning of September twenty ninth 1940. During those days it was customary for pregnant single parents to rush into marriage, to cover up their imaginary misdeed, to appease the wrath of pious, self-created, self-appointed little Gods, or to prevent a vile stigma from being attached to an innocent child. It was an attitude imposed by religious fanatics and false religions and non-religious frauds. It might truthfully have been said that it was religion which had first done its best to utilise and exploit me, and to be the first to condemn me. In consequence of this it should suprise no-one that I was not under the spell of any religion.

My experience of life had taught me to become more mundane and practical. My child had already been born out of wedlock, and that could not be changed. Many of the nicest people on this earth have been conceived out of wedlock, among them Jesus Himself, the Man claimed by so many to have been the Son of God, the Man that so many people claim to follow and worship. I cannot recall having heard anyone condemn either God or Joseph or whoever begat Jesus out of wedlock or condemn Mary for having been sexually indulgent. I cannot recall having heard anyone condemn the Psalmist for his sexual aggression and for begetting so many children out of wedlock. If it was acceptable for God and the Psalmist to beget children outside of wedlock why was it not acceptable for me to do the same? No one can deny that wedlock is a highly desirable institution or state, designed and created by man for the healthy, orderly procreation of man, for the security, for the raising and for the training of children in an affectionate, stable, secure, happy and harmonious atmosphere, provided and secured by both parents. That is not to say that a single parent cannot or does not bring up children as well, and sometimes better than some married couples. Single parents often do better. In the eyes of the virtuous, wedlock also legalizes and normalizes their own sexual indulgences whether for the purpose of procreation, or for their own mutual sexual lust or gratification. A farmer with three sons, all of which I knew well, required his sons to work before going to school in the mornings, and after they returned home in the evenings.

In addition they were required to rush home in the school's dinner break, bolt down their dinner, and muck out the cow sheds before again returning to their lessons. This farmer took his dinner with him when he worked in the fields, he ate his food as he ploughed. He owned and farmed two hundred acres. His sons left school to work for their father under the same conditions as our family. He told them in no uncertain terms that if they did get a girl into trouble all they would obtain from him would be a hundred pounds and the door. I obtained the equivalent of the door, but through patience and endurance received rather more than one hundred pounds. These three boys never did cause their parents any heartache, as far as I know.

Those were the good old days of yesteryear.

CHAPTER 6

Farming for War
1939 – 1944

From the day I became partner in the business, I took complete charge of the cheque book. While I had been in full charge of the business for many years before this, my business expertise had been seriously restricted through the unavailability of the financial balance sheet and the cheque book. I had been farming and planning in the dark. I had no idea what money was available with which to trade.

While previously my father had made out all the cheques himself, the only information that I received from him was when I purchased stock or materials. He would frequently tell me that there was no money to pay for them, but I cautiously carried on albeit blindly. With access to the cheque book and the balance sheet, I was in a far better position to manage. I was able to make the fullest use of the time at my disposal. Fortunately, for me 1941 proved a good year for animal farming, also for harvesting the hay and cereals. The weather for the 1941 harvest proved much better than did the weather for the few following harvests. During the autumn of 1940 we had planted a substantial acreage to winter wheat. My father's youngest brother Edmund arrived at Molenick Farm one morning after the wheat had been cut and stooked. He said to me, 'John, this is like olden times.' During Uncle Edmund's olden times, a good crop of wheat yielded around one ton to the acre, when the 1941 wheat crop was threshed it had yielded two tons to the acre. Our sons are now producing yields of up to four tons to the acre. The present heavier yields are obtained partly from higher yielding strains or varieties, partly from the control of wheat diseases, and partly from applying higher rates of nitrogen.

The 1941 hay crop was cut and stacked during three weeks of perfect weather. Plenty of labour was available, and a standard Fordson tractor which we had purchased eighteen months earlier swept the hay to the ricks. We had also adapted the tractor to pull the finger bar grass mower to cut some of the hay, to ease the horses. I usually placed four men on the hay rick. I handled the hay grab myself, one man led the horse for the hay grab, one man swept the hay to the rick at top speed with the tractor, and one man raked the hay field with a horse rake.

With this team we ricked twenty five tons on the last day of the fine weather in the last field of hay to be carried, between 1.30 p.m. and 7 p.m. I drove those men hard.

One of the first binders in the parish with John Wills, tenant of 304-acre Trehunsey, in the driver's seat. His men were still nervous of the 'new-fangled machinery' so he, himself, cut other farmers' corn for 2s. 6d. per acre. Reg Wills, his young son, is on horseback and (left) Mr Higman, grandfather of Mrs Welch (see helpers) holds a sheaf of wheat. All the farming photographs were taken between 1895 and 1905

Jim, who had just turned fifty, said to me one morning towards the end of the harvest 'It's alright for you, Jack, you are young and fit, you can stick it. The pace you are setting is bloody nigh killing me.'

We threshed the spring corn at harvest time. We covered the wheat ricks with sheets of galvanised iron to thresh them later. Ten acres of potatoes were stored and I bagged them and weighed them myself later. The farm's sale of live and dead stock was held on the 23rd September 1941, surprisingly, perhaps without a single regret. My young life was nearing the end of one chapter. By the time the wheat had been threshed and sold and paid for, by the time the potatoes had been cleared, January 1942 had arrived. By the time everything had been wound up I had repaid the mortgage of two thousand and nine hundred pounds owing on Venn Farm and the cottages, leaving a balance of four thousand pounds remaining after the balance had been paid off. My partnership with my father related only to his business at Molenick Farm and did not include his stake in Venn Farm, in which case the mortgage on that farm had not been my personal responsibility. My partnership with my father had entitled me to redeem the mortgage, and one-half of the balance of four thousand pounds which meant one-half of six thousand and nine hundred pounds or three thousand and four hundred and fifty pounds.

Having been eager to play fair, and eager not to give any one of the family the slightest opportunity of accusing me of being selfish, I took nothing from the two thousand and nine hundred pounds, but took two thousand pounds from the four thousand pounds. I gave my parents two thousand pounds in cash. I had estimated that the two thousand pounds would have been somewhere near my entitlement for eighteen and a half years service and management of Molenick Farm. I was quite happy with this reward if I could also obtain the tenancy of Venn Farm. The ownership of a one hundred and seventy five acre farm, plus two cottages, plus two thousand pounds in cash, had placed my parents in a very respectable independent financial position. At 1985 prices, the equivalent value would be over three hundred and fifty thousand pounds today. I had given my brother Hedley the cheques, the bank statements, and the accounts relating to the period when I had been a partner, to acquaint him with the general financial situation, and also to prove the amount of cash I had taken from my parent's estate. I suppose it is only natural for everyone to imagine that they have done the correct and honourable thing, and which, seemingly, entitles them to any favours floating around as flotsam. I had also imagined that I had been unselfish and devoted to the cause, which entitled me to ask my father if I could move into Venn Farm and set up business there, to which he readily consented. It was not possible for any person with such a small amount of capital to farm this size of property, unless, or until, the owner has sufficient confidence in, and is willing to trust that person with possession of his property. In my case the availability of Venn Farm, plus my father's (the rightful owner) permission to farm it, was, in money terms, a great asset and worth a great deal.

Having said that, a Mr Stanley Betty, who with his brother William owned several farms but owed me nothing, approached me before I left Molenick Farm and said to me, 'If ever you want a farm to work, I will willingly provide you with one.' I thanked him for his very sincere offer. Although the tenant of Venn Farm was generally acknowledged to have been a poor farmer, I did not wish to turn him out of the farm if there was an alternative. The tenant farmer was a married man about sixty years old with no family. I tried for some little time to persuade him to take me into partnership when one of us could, in due course, have obtained a second farm to move into. As it transpired I should have presented him a notice to quit at Ladyday, 1942, and sorted out the partnership business one way or the other afterwards, and I tried not to be callous or inconsiderate. It came about that the tenant, not unnaturally, delayed his final reply until after Ladyday, 1942. The farm being on a Ladyday take, I had to wait until Ladyday 1943, before I could present him with a twelve month's notice to vacate at Ladyday 1944. During November 1943, the Government stepped in, and ordered everyone with their entire belongings to vacate the area by the following twentieth December. The American Armed Forces were to take over the area for use as a battle training area in preparation for D-Day and the invasion of France. The area consisted of about two hundred farms including Venn Farm and the villages of Blackawton, East Allington,

Slapton Sands, Start Bay on the South Devon coast, picture taken from Torcross.
Extending nearly three miles, the beach was used as a landing area behind shellfire from ships in the bay.
This part of South Devon was used as a battle training area by American Armed Forces in preparation for D-Day.
It was on and off this beach on the 27th and 28th April 1944 that around 1000 Americans lost their lives. While the American ships lying in the bay dropped their shells short or the troops had advanced too soon on the night of the 27th, on the night of the 28th enemy torpedo boats sank several landing craft during Operation Tiger.
The Sherman tank (inset) was raised from the bed of the bay.
The land behind the bay is where my Uncle Tom, Aunt Kate and my cousins once farmed, Stokeley Barton.
Ven is situated at about the centre of the top of the picture from where the sands can be seen

Frogmore, Chillington, Strete, Sherford, Slapton, Stokenham, and many private houses. Venn Farm is situated on the second hill inland from Slapton Sands, a stretch of sands some two and a half miles long, situated in Start Bay, lying between Start Point and Froward Point at the mouth of the River Dart, on the South coast of Devon. Here American servicemen were required to land repeatedly on the sands by day and by night, from landing craft, to advance inland behind and under a barrage of shellfire provided by American ships lying in the Bay.

One dreadful night 27th April, 1944 a number of American servicemen lost their lives through enemy action while on exercise in the Bay. It was recorded that the number of casualties exceeded seven hundred and forty nine. The fields and the woods around Venn Farm were riddled with shell holes. Several unexploded shells have since been ploughed up on Venn Farm. When a Naval bomb disposal officer came to detonate one live shell that Les Pengelly had ploughed up, Les said to him, 'Suppose I had been blown up?' The Naval man replied, 'What is one among so many?' Les didn't think that was funny. It was considered that more American servicemen were killed while training in the area than were killed on the Normandy beaches on D-Day. A field adjoining Narramore Cross, near Venn Farm was used as a field hospital for treating casualties. When we were permitted to enter Venn Farm during October 1944, the place resembled a wilderness. Grass meadows were full of grass and thistles, stubble fields were full of weeds and the swede, turnip and kale fields had gone to seed. One field was red, on first sight we thought it had been ploughed. On closer inspection we discovered that it was docks that had gone to seed. Strange to relate, this field had not produced a single dock plant since. Tanks had crossed and recrossed the farm fields and the farm fences. Gun pits, slit trenches, rifle ammunition, T.N.T., full tins of bully beef, and tins of soup abounded. The whole area was infested with rats. On the first evening I was there, I stood on one spot in the farm yard with a club. I struck down rats as fast as I could strike as they milled around me, without moving an inch, until I became bored and tired. I plastered the farm buildings with poison every evening. For the first six nights all the poison was taken, on the seventh night a little poison was left.

While in Tideford Village I did a turn with the Home Guard, we went into the village most nights. One night I was on guard at Tideford, someone telephoned my mother and said, 'Send John out to extinguish the incendiaries around your house and in your fields.' She told her, 'John is not here.' The lady said, 'Where is he?' My mother said, 'Out guarding you.' The Home Guard had been in existence for more than twelve months when Sid Screech, one of our company died. The committal service was on a Sunday. Home Guards were instructed to attend in their uniforms. Every Home Guard attended in uniform, with the exception of one of our Lieutenants who wore mufti. As I had never seen this man in uniform I regarded this as being rather out of place when he took his turn carrying the coffin with uniformed members. The following Sunday evening we assembled at our post to take night shift. When one of the other three Home Guards said that this Lieutenant would be inspecting the guard during the night, I said, 'If he inspects me in mufti I will put him off the post.' They said, 'You won't.' I assured them that I would. Later that night, when I was off duty in the shed I heard one of the boys say, 'Good evening, Mr Banbury.' At first I assumed that they were pulling my leg, then I heard fresh voices. I picked up my rifle, buttoned up my coat, and moved outside where Mr Banbury was talking to my mates. I said, 'Good evening, Mr Banbury, I must advise you that this is a military post where civilians are not welcome. I would appreciate it if you would retrace your steps the way you came.' He was a gentleman farmer who always carried a walking stick. He commenced circling the walking stick in the palm of his hand, he did not move his feet. I repeated my request. He still swung his stick but he did not move a foot. I brought my rifle to attention, I slowly walked into him and pushed him with my chest back and down the lane the way he came. My mates were struck dumb. The following morning a Home Guard Sergeant arrived at my home to take a statement. I asked, 'What did my mates say?' He said that they saw nothing. I said, 'That's fair enough. They were not involved in any way.' The Sergeant said, 'The Lieutenant wants you courtmartialled.' I said, 'I have never seen him in uniform, I had no reason for believing that he was a Lieutenant in the Home Guard, if he is prepared to inspect me in a Lieutenant's uniform he will obtain from me the respect to which the uniform is entitled.' I never received an official reply but I know that he resigned from the Home Guard.

During the time of the Home Guard Molenick Farm possessed the only telephone in the area North of Tideford including Tideford Cross. We took all the Home Guard messages for the area and I delivered the messages on my motor cycle.

A message came through at one a.m. for every Home Guard to assemble at base 'pronto'. I dressed, jumped on my motor cycle and set off. I called Fred Gimblett at Trewolsta, who had only recently married , first of all, and told him that I would call the others and return for him. After calling the others I returned to Trewolsta, expecting Fred to be ready.

The light was still showing in Fred's bedroom. I shouted, 'Come on, Fred.' He shouted back, 'I'm coming, Jack.' The light remained on in the bedroom, no light had appeared anywhere else in the house. I kept shouting at Fred, he answered me every time, but the light did not leave Fred's bedroom for a considerable time. I eventually got a bit wicked, I said, 'Fred, they will have been and gone again before we get there if you don't hurry.' He still shouted back, 'I'm coming, Jack.' When he did eventually arrive and had seated himself behind me on my motor cycle, I said to him, 'Wouldn't Annie let you go?' He said 'It wasn't that, Jack, you will never believe me when I tell you.' I said 'Try me.' Fred said 'I couldn't find my braces.' I said 'You couldn't go without your braces, Fred?' He said 'I knew you wouldn't believe me.' In the hustle the braces became mixed up with the bedclothes. We turned the clothes over and over again. We knew they must be there somewhere, but find them we couldn't.' I said 'Perhaps Annie didn't want to find them.' Fred said 'I knew that you wouldn't believe me.'

Evelyn's brother Ern was Sergeant of a Bethany Home Guard section. They were called out the same night as we were, and some of the Bethany Home Guards were stationed at cross roads in pairs. A man named Mackie was standing motionless at one cross road when a small animal suddenly rustled some dry leaves in the hedge, which frightened Mackie who instantly emptied a rifle shell at the hedge from whence came the rustle. Hedley was Sergeant to a Blunts section. I joined Liskeard Home Guard when I moved to Liskeard and became a member of the spigot mortar anti-tank team.

I knew the first person to be killed in Plymouth blitz. He was a Mr Slee who kept a butchers' shop in Marlborough Street, Devonport, along which we passed every week. I also carry a vivid recollection of having seen the first bombs that fell on Plymouth leave the enemy plane. From Saltash on a brilliantly clear day I saw the bombs glisten in the sun as they left the high flying plane, but I did not see the bombs falling.

However, there is something missing or unreal in this mental picture: the absence of the balloons which usually rose high over Plymouth during the war years which casts doubts on the authenticity of this mental picture. I have asked myself was this perhaps one of my vivid dreams, or was it real? Up until now I have been unable to answer this question.

While farming itself is often glorified, glamourised and adorned with the most beautiful sentiments by everyone but the farmer, for some mysterious reason maybe from jealousy, maybe because they wear baggy trousers, or maybe because they have acquired the image of being straw suckers with grass growing from their ears, farmers are still being regarded as serfs by the superior city dweller.

During the blitz on Plymouth by the Luftwaffe in the early 1940's a Plymouth family of, at least, four generations arrived at Molenick Farm late one night to enquire if we would permit them to spend the remainder of the night in one of our straw barns. The family consisted of a lady in her eighties, her son about sixty, and younger people, mainly females, and small children. I said, 'We can do better than that for you. We have an empty dwelling at Kilquite House a quarter of a mile down the road, where we could provide you with mattresses, blankets, black outs and oil lamps.' They accepted. The night was black as pitch. I put a horse in a cart and took the mattresses, the blankets and all the necessary items to make them comfortable and settled them in. Kilquite House was about ten miles by road form the centre of Plymouth. The family stayed there for about three weeks. After they had been at the house for about a week the active sixty year old man came running to me across the field shouting, 'Farmer, farmer.' as if in distress. I turned my footsteps in his direction. When he came close he said, 'Will you empty our bucket?' I said, 'Pardon?' 'Will you empty our bucket for us?' I said, 'What bucket?' He said 'The bucket in the little house in the garden.' I said, 'Why do you want that bucket emptied?' He said, 'Because it's full.' I said, 'But you can do that little job yourself.' He said, 'I can't.' I said, 'Well, I could, and I would had it been necessary. As you are an active man I do not consider it necessary that I should do so.' He said, 'Then what are we to do?' I said, 'The same as country people have done all through the ages, use the garden or the fields.' I left him standing there still very worried. I later made it my business to find out what happened. It transpired that 'Granny', the old lady emptied the bucket.

We never enquired their names, their addresses, their occupation, or their life styles, they never told us. They disappeared into the night as silently as they had arrived. We required no thanks, we received no thanks.

Before mod-cons became the fashion, latrines, locally known as closets or lavatories, were usually situated in the garden. They may have been built of stone, brick or wood. Seats consisted of a long plank of wood with several holes cut to fit the size of the user's bottoms.

When visiting one house Geoff and Clarence passed the closet where Mr and Mrs (huge persons) were observed seated meditating side by side on this plank with the door wide open.

In a hamlet not far from here a wood closet stood in the garden with its back against another garden. A board or two had fallen off its back where the nails had rusted through. Young Jack had seen an old lady enter the closet after dark, he could do nothing better than to grab a bunch of stinging nettles and plunge them through the gap left by the fallen boards.

As a boy while working in our field I have seen poor old crippled Ned Fowel enter his wooden closet on a bitterly cold March morning and heard him groan in pain for some little while before seeing him emerge. Many of those old people lived hard and died hard. Current humans are not appreciative of the benefits they are receiving from modern comforts or from the advanced science of medicine.

My father must have been around 44 years of age when I was born. I cannot remember my father walking without the assistance of a stick to support his lame leg. He had paid specialists hundreds of pounds over a period of years to diagnose the ailment and to suggest treatment. The specialists' conclusions were that our father was suffering from sciatica, which when translated means neuralgia in the hip nerve and that is usually a very painful condition.

When I was small my father sometimes took me with him when he visited a specialist in the Mannamead area of Plymouth. Over the years this diagnosed sciatica became progressively worse in the left hip, and the complaint in due course spread to the hip on his right side, when he required a stick in each hand to assist him to walk. His walking speed slowed until he could move his feet forward no more than a few inches at a time.

I remember returning home for lunch one day when mother said 'I have not seen dad for some time, you had better look around for him.' I eventually found him lying on the barn floor, quite some distance from the farmhouse. He had fallen when his feet became tangled in some straw and he couldn't rise without assistance. He was lying in the dry straw and seemed amused and said he knew someone would 'happen along eventually'.

It had been only a matter of time before he was confined to a wheelchair, from which he had to be lifted in and lifted out.

We moved to Newhouse Farm, Liskeard, with May and Louis at Michaelmas 1941, when father was about 75 years of age. Newhouse Farm was some distance from the doctor who had been attending father for the previous 16 years, so my mother called in a medical practitioner from Liskeard to give dad a thorough examination to cover any eventuality. The doctor arrived one day when I was away at work.

When I returned home mother said 'Doctor Metcalf has been today to examine dad.' She added that she had told the doctor she thought dad was suffering from sciatica but that he had suggested he might be suffering from creeping paralysis. I said 'Mum, Doctor Metcalf appears to me to have been talking sense.' Mother said 'How do you make that out?' I said 'Apart from dad's sister Hannah having contracted rheumatic fever, there is no rheumatism to be found anywhere in his family. Where there is rheumatism there is always pain. Sciatica is rheumatism to the hips, as arthritis is rheumatism to the wrists and to the ankles. Dad has never suffered the slightest pain, he eats well, and he sleeps more than is normal, otherwise he is perfectly healthy. He has always been in good bodily condition.'

I had been suprised that dad's three medical advisers, who had attended him since the specialist diagnosed sciatica, had accepted the specialist's diagnosis without question. I was a mere layman, but I knew that where there is rheumatism there is pain. What had I been thinking about, what had these three medical practitioners been thinking about when they examined him? The germ which causes creeping paralysis can apparently be found in dust or in mould, found in materials such as hay or corn or in old buildings, actually anywhere. It apparently enters the body through the respiratory tract.

May and her husband Louis had very kindly permitted my parents and myself to share their farmhouse at Newhouse, Lamellion, Liskeard between leaving Molenick Farm and moving into Venn Farm. Louis and May were two peace-loving people, they had never been known to become involved in a confrontation with anyone. To fill in my time after the wheat and potatoes had been cleared, I worked for the Cornwall War Agricultural Executive Committee, driving one of a fleet of Fordson Standard tractors stationed at St Neot and managed by Mr John Horton. I commenced working with this Standard Fordson tractor trailing a Lister Cockshut plough, ploughing an eighteen acre field one Monday morning on a farm not far from St Neot village. The farmer had been a big noise in the area having been a prizewinning horse ploughman, a keen horse showman, and a judge at many agricultural functions. The farmer had come to work in the same field, near to where I was working, at about crib time. Not having partaken of my mid-morning snack, I jumped off my tractor with my snack bag not far from where the farmer had commenced working. I had knelt on my hat with one knee on the soil and had attempted to open my lunch-bag when he rushed towards me thrusting a four-pronged dung fork menacingly at my chest as if to stab me, stopping only when the tool was no more than an inch from my chest. He then withdrew the four-pronged fork, and plunged it into the ground between us, jumping up and down like a yo-yo. I looked up above me, thinking perhaps it was his intention to impress me with his vaulting prowess. After completing his exhibition, he shouted, 'Who is paying for

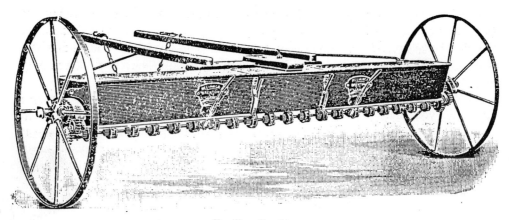

Fertiliser distributor
Its heyday, latter half of nineteenth and the first half of the twentieth century

the time you are stopped now?' I instantly reflected that having slaved for my first employer for seventeen years before receiving recognition, now my second employer, an obvious tyrant, would have refused me time to eat. The exhibition was so ludicrous that I instantly burst out laughing in his face which was, by now, quite close to mine. If the man had been seeking a battle he was doomed to disappointment, for I completely ignored his outburst. He returned to his work. I completed my lunch. Just for devilment I said, 'Mr West, I am partial to a jug of hot tea with my lunch, if there is one available.' He sent one of his regular employees with a jug of tea for my mid-day meal every day of the week after that little episode.

On the Wednesday morning I moved a few rabbit gins before going to work. He was after me, he said, 'You are late for work.' I replied, 'I understand that you pay six shillings an hour for every hour worked. If I am not working for you, you are not paying. As it happened I did move some rabbit gins this morning, but this is really no business of yours.' On the Friday I asked the employee who brought the tea if the boss had made any comments. He said that the boss had told him that I did more work before lunch than his regular workers did all week. This disgruntled man also remarked that they could not understand their boss sending me tea every day as it would be a waste of time for any of the regulars to request even a glass of water. From these remarks, I decided it was time for me to move on to another farm. I worked all day on the Saturday. On the Monday morning the boss was waiting for me. He was ready with his orders. I said, 'Thank you, Mr West, but I must be on the move, we have to spread our help among as many as we can.' I moved to a field adjoining the same farm for a Mr Dawe, if my memory is correct. The condition of the soil in this field was such that I was able to plough at speed. Moving quite fast over this level field during the afternoon I felt the back end of the tractor drop then rise again. I turned my head to notice a large hole appear where I had just worked.

The tractor's spade lug wheels had managed to pull the tractor and the plough out from what could have been a nasty hole large enough to have swallowed the tractor, the plough, and myself up, quite easily. I did not stop to investigate the depth of the hole. It had been a mining area and it was probably due to the collapse of a mining adit.

For twelve months I ploughed land, disc-harrowed land, drilled corn, cut corn with a binder and dug out potatoes with a tractor potato digger, from Liskeard to Cheesewring, to Bolventor and Daphne Du Maurier's famous Jamaica Inn, to well beyond Bodmin Road Station, at Boconnoc, to Greymare, The Taphouses and wherever in all weathers. I have been ploughing high up on Wardbrook when it has been sleeting and freezing, when my clothes became as stiff as a board, when it became dangerous to attend to the calls of nature. I ploughed only a little virgin land on Bodmin Moor, which was at Blisland.

The C.A.E.C. charged six shillings an hour for the work I did with the tractor and implements. Having been stuck in one rut on one farm for so long, it was quite an experience to work on so many farms and to observe so many types and conditions of farming. The only confrontation that I experienced during the twelve months occurred on the morning that I commenced working for the Committee. I found everyone else very pleasant.

At around the time that I commenced working for Mr John Horton at St. Neot, I approached a member of the Cornwall W.A.E.C. living near Liskeard whom I had never met before, with a view to ascertaining the possibility of obtaining a tractor, a plough and a disc harrow for contracting on my own, and in due course working on Venn Farm. The destination of all available tractors, ploughs, disc harrows and other machinery was entirely at the discretion of the Committee. Twelve months later I visited this gentleman again at his home, to again enquire if there was any likelihood of me obtaining the tractor and the implements.

The C.W.A.E.C. provided me with a tractor and a plough within a couple of weeks and I commenced agricultural contracting on my own account on March 1st, 1943. The tractor was kept working all the hours of daylight, and often more.

I commenced working at eight o'clock one morning and continued ploughing by moonlight until three thirty the following morning. The air had become very cold, and the tractor had no lights. During the first three weeks of its life, this tractor consumed one hundred and eighty gallons of T.V.O. each week, using a gallon and a half of T.V.O. an hour while the dry spell lasted. A notice to vacate Venn Farm at Ladyday, 1944 was delivered to the tenant before noon on Ladyday, 1943.

VIVERDON DOWN

Viverdon Down and Amy Down extended to some six hundred and forty six acres,

Combined seed and fertiliser drill
Its heyday latter part of nineteenth and the first half of the twentieth centuries

Grass mower
Its heyday, latter part of nineteenth and the first half of the twentieth centuries

Hay pole with guy ropes and grab
Its heyday first half of twentieth century.

Cousin John horse raking a barley stubble overlooking Slapton Ley, Slapton Sands and Start Bay, on
Stokeley Barton Farm, Stokenham, Nr. Kingsbridge, during the nineteen twenties

Threshing: Early 1920s scene using the straw 'lifter' or elevator (far left). The ladies on the left have just arrived with the croust. Note the boys pouring water into the engine's tender.

This was the first car ever seen in Quethiock, AF17 a Sunbeam registered by W. Coryton on August 8th 1906. It had come to the village to pick up members of a shooting party who were taking late refreshments at East Quethiock Farm. The villagers gathered around this new monster and hitherto accustomed to trap-lamps were astounded by the powerful head lights

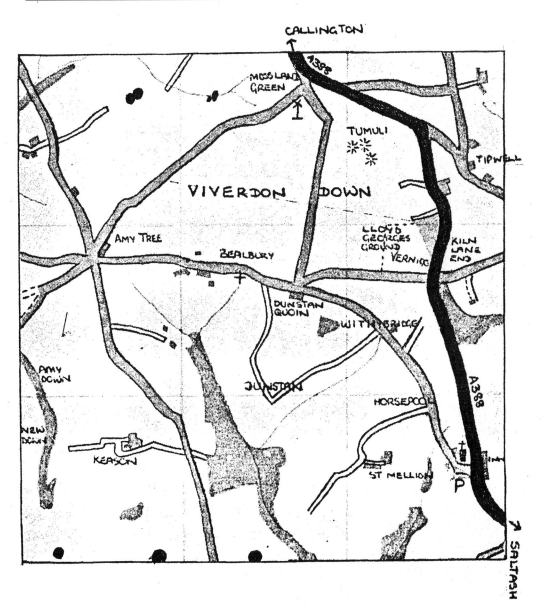

Map of Viverdon

about eighty acres of which was Amy Down. Viverdon Down rose gently to six hundred and sixty feet above sea level; it commands marvellous views of the countryside, almost all around it, but especially over the River Tamar to Plymouth and to the English Channel. Even so, the view cannot compare with the view from the top of the nearby one thousand pinnacle at Kit Hill or the Cheesewring at

A corn harvesting scene on Viverdon during the late eighteen nineties

Minions from where on a clear day it is possible to look over the distant county of Devon into Somerset. Squire William Goryton, owner of Pentille Castle and estate bordering the River Tamar for several miles and covering several villages inland, commenced the mammoth task of cleaning and ploughing this area of virgin land during 1893 to provide work for some of the thousand out-of-work miners when the Great Consols mining operation at Calstock and Morwellham came to the end of its career.

Viverdon Down was covered in gorse and bracken with some clumps of willow (withy) and hazel (nuttal). The Down also contained some deep bogs. Pipes were laid five feet deep, the collected water was used to drive two hydrams which pumped water into two reservoirs. A windmill supplemented the two rams. The gorse willow and hazel were cut and bound into faggots, which together with small stones were placed around and over the pipes which drained the bogs. These faggots still survive in reasonable condition after almost a century. The Down had harboured rabbits and hares, pheasants and partridges.

This area was ploughed by large prairie buster type ploughs which required eight horses to pull each plough. One of these three ploughs stood at the blacksmith's shop at Pillaton until we left during 1925. This plough probably went for scrap to support the Second War effort. John Smale Drown was succeeded by a Mr Richard Drown. I well remember refusing to accept a penny piece which Mr Richard Drown had offered me one Sunday evening in the road outside Trewashford garden gate

Uncle John with beard on horse nearest camera talking to followers at a coursing meeting on Viverdon

during 1913. Viverdon land contained many stones and rocks which were picked. The large stones were used for building hedges, the smaller stones were used for making more that two miles of new roads. Strict hedge building specifications were laid down by the squire. The base of the hedge must not be less than six feet wide, the height of the stonework not less than four feet and six inches and topped with earth. The top width of the hedge to be not less than two feet and nine inches. Beech and thorn were planted on top of the hedge.

The hedges appear in as good condition as they were when they were first built. However, the hedges do not appear as high to my eye today as they did seventy years ago at the end of the nineteenth century when these hedges were made. Married workers received fifteen shillings (equal to seventy five pence today) for a six day, fifty or fifty four hour week. Piece-work was available for hedge building at a rate of two shillings and six pence (equal today thirteen pence) for building a sixteen and a half feet length of hedge, known as a Land Yard which should not be confused with a yard of land measuring sixteen and a half feet by sixteen and a half feet. There are one hundred and sixty yards of land in an acre. There are one hundred and sixty stone a ton. So, one stone per yard equals one ton per acre.

Lloyd George's land was drained and the water taken to Crocadon Farm where it was used to drive a Water wheel.

It was at that time that Lloyd George as Chancellor of the Exchequer levied a

Land Enclosure Tax. This tax put an abrupt end to the Squire's reclamation work and before this part of the Down was reclaimed. It was the locals who christened this — this uncultivated land – Lloyd George's Land.

Amy Down was ploughed and brought into cultivation during the Second World War. Viverdon Down in due course produced good crops of oats and of hay.

On one occasion, more than a hundred Pentille estate workers were seen working in one fifty acre hay field. Some were turning hay with forks by hand. Some were collecting hay with two horse hay sweeps. Some were stacking hay into four large hay stacks using hay poles with hay grabs and with elevators.

The Down played its part producing and providing oats and hay for the Army horses of the First World War.

It was over the newly cultivated virgin land at Viverdon that my Uncle John, a Pentille estate tenant farming Bealbury Farm with permission from the Squire and from the estate tenants arranged and mastered three hare coursing meetings each winter. Hare coursing on Viverdon and on Westcot Farm — owned by Messrs. Peter and Pete Hambly — was a strictly private affair. Attendance was by invitation only.

I recently inherited a suitably inscribed silver salver which had been presented to Uncle John by hare coursing followers. It was dated 1911. The photograph is a corn harvesting scene near Viverdon Cottages from one of Viverdon Down's first corn crops at the end of the last century.

Bealbury Methodist Church
Centenary Celebrations
1872 – 1972
April 29th – 30th

A Methodist Church was built on land close by Bealbury Bridge during 1872.

The land was given by Miss Jennifer Hodge of Bealbury.

The church cost £300 to build.

This wayside Bethel supported by country folk is still very much alive while the Bethel at Pillaton surrounded by a far more affluent society has been dead for many years.

EDMUND GREET

My mother's uncle Edmund retired from farming Wisewandra Farm, of approaching two hundred acres, around 1925.

On retirement he retained three fields, and built a house in one of these fields called Pinglestone. Many years earlier when he moved to Wisewandra Farm he possessed very little money. When he sent his horseman Dick Sutch to commence ploughing during his first autumn at Wisewandra, he said to Sutch, 'Plough as

Bealbury Methodist Church

Bealbury Farmhouse built about 1866

shallow as you possibly can this year, as I can't afford to buy any fertiliser.'

When he sent Sutch out to plough during the second autumn of his stay at Wisewandra, my great uncle said to his man, 'I still can't afford to buy any fertiliser, you must plough an inch deeper this year to make up for this.' This went on for a few autumns, each autumn Sutch was told to plough an inch deeper to make up for the lack of fertiliser, until one autumn, when on his return from the first morning's ploughing Edmund asked Sutch how things were going. Sutch replied, 'You've had your last ruddy inch this time boss, you will be forced to buy some fertiliser next year.' Uncle Edmund was rather short in stature, he was quite dandy, upright as a bolt, his goat beard was neatly trimmed to a point at the chin. He often visited Molenick, driving a smart horse and a rubber-tyred gig.

On a visit for tea, one afternoon, after he had reached the age of eighty years, when he had seated himself at the table, he said to mother, 'Mary, I am getting married again.' Without replying mother left the table to attend to the cooking on the stove, on her return Uncle Edmund said again, 'Mary, I am getting married.' Mother went in search of another job without replying, on her return to the table again Edmund, in a more subdued voice, said again, 'Mary, I am getting married.' Mother said to him, 'Don't talk so silly.' His face commencing to beam again he said, 'But I am.' Mother said, 'Who in the world would want to marry you?' Edmund, his face now fairly beaming, replied, 'Miss Goldy.' Mother queried with a puzzled look, 'And how old would she be?' Stroking his beardy chin he replied, 'Thirty six.' Edmund duly married his lady love. They buried him nine weeks to the day he was married.

While living at Wisewandra, Edmund had occasion to ride horseback to Pillaton one dark, wild and stormy winter's evening. On returning home late it was so dark beneath the trees at the Torr end of Clapper Bridge Road, that Edumund gave his horse the reins for the horse to pick his own way home. Running along by the side of the road was a Mill Leat, between the Mill Leat and the River Lynher was very boggy ground. It happened just a couple of hundred yards or so upstream from where Mr Hands, the East Cornwall Hunt's whip, was washed off his horse on New Year's Day 1914. Edmund's horse very soon walked or fell into the Mill Leat, throwing Edmund onto the bank on the other side of the Leat. The sound of a waterfall a few yards away, plus the sound of the fast flowing river, contributed to a weird situation. It was so dark that he was afraid to move an inch.

This happened several years before the advent of the motor car, and it was unlikely anybody would be passing at that time of night, but Edmund could whistle loudly with his fingers to his lips, so he kept whistling. Tommy Manuel's wife happened to be going into her dairy of their cottage called 'Enquire The Way' which was situated about a mile upstream from where uncle was trapped, and intended to retire for the night. The window of the dairy faced down stream. She heard Uncle Edmund whistling, and after much thought had decided that it came from someone in trouble. However, she had great difficulty in persuading her husband, Tom, to take a lantern, and turn out on such a night to go in search of the unusual calling. But, eventually they came across Uncle Edmund and were able to release him. He was usually of a jovial disposition, perky as a bantam cock and full of fun, but there was not much fun around that cold, wet night. He and his first wife Fanny were affectionately known to the whole of the Parish and beyond, young and old, they all called them, Cocky Greet and Fartin Fanny.

Maggie Manuel was the one who told me of the local lad who lived near, 'Enquire the Way' who took her sister for a walk one summer's evening. Although they enjoyed a long casual stroll around the shire lanes, all he said during the whole of the time was, 'Butter has gone up.' And as they neared the homestead he again ventured, 'Eggs have gone down.' At the end of the evening on her doorstep, when he found more courage to ask her when they could meet her again, the girl said sardonically, 'When eggs go up and when butter comes down.' Life can become terribly, terribly tough.

WILLIAM TIPPET

It is normal to meet a few rare characters during one's lifetime. One such was a Mr William (Bill) Tippet. He was married, childless, owner-occupier of around four hundred acre Holwood Farm situated one mile from Molenick Farm until about 1943. Bill was a tall, gaunt man who was addicted to his pipe, to the extent that, he would partake of a 'draw' or two during the night. Bill always commenced a sentence with the expression 'I main (mean).' When he met another pipe smoker, he would feel around his pockets for the larger of his two pipes he carried around and say, ' 'ave e got a bit'o baccy?' If anyone was foolish enough to say 'Yes.' He would produce and set about stuffing the extra large bowled pipe as tightly as he could with tobacco, after which he would pretend to search for matches then say, ' 'ave e got a match to spare?'

Bill employed ten men, he once said to me, 'I 'main', Jack, I tell my men to do one thing an' I 'main' they'll go right and do something else.' When Bill was inspecting his livestock on horseback, he would drop in to any one of his neighbour's houses, pull up a chair, in front of the open fire or stove, put his feet on the mantle shelf, smoke his pipe, spit in the fire, and break wind almost non-stop.

Bill was not a prompt payer.

During one very wet day during August 1941, I had made out some business accounts and was taking letters to post at Tideford Cross on the motor cycle. Not far from the Post Office letter box, was a clean area where the Council stored chippings and where formerly stone-breakers broke stones for the Parish roads. Bill had been seated in his Austin Seven car. He saw me coming, he jumped out of his car, came towards me and said, 'I 'main', Jack, youm the man I'm looking for. I 'main' I've got a puncture. I've been her since ten o'clock' I said, 'There is a garage at Tideford.'

He complained, 'I sent down and asked someone to come up this morning. I 'main' no one has arrived.' I said, 'I'll post these letters first.' Bill said, ' 'ave e got a spare stamp?' I said, 'What do you want the stamp for? To mend the puncture?' Bill laughed and said, 'I 'main', darn thou, Jack.' Fred Gimblett arrived soon after this to post his letter. I told him, pointing to the broken-down car, 'Fred, the 'ol man is in trouble.' Fred answered helpfully, 'I'll give you a hand after I've posted these letters.' With the puncture repaired, Bill tried to start the motor again and again. Bill said, 'Will you boys give me a push?' Fred and I were big enough fools to push him some distance along the road. Ultimately, I said to Fred, 'The 'ol Devil has taken out the rotor arm and hasn't put it back. Stop, Fred.' Bill shouted to us to keep pushing, but I shouted back, 'We've finished.' Bill cajoled, 'I 'main' I'll give you a drink sometime.' But I told him that we'd heard that one before, he knew I didn't drink anyway. So, after a bit of 'argy-bargy' I told him, 'Look, farmer, put back the rotor arm and see if that will make any difference.' He fairly shouted, 'I 'main' I've not taken out the rotor arm.' But I insisted that he take a look under the bonnet. He got out of the car, lifted the bonnet and said, 'I 'main', Jack, you was right.'

During 1938, Bill came to Molenick and asked me, 'I 'main', Jack, 'ave 'e got any oats to spare for my horses?' I said, 'I'm afraid we haven't Mr Tippet.' He said, 'I 'main', Jack, I know you have, because you threshed some oats last week.' 'We will need these for our own horses.' I explained, trying to fob him off.

He hung around and badgered me so long, that, in the end, I said, 'You can have ten hundred weight.' He never paid for those oats.

We left Molenick in 1941. Bill left Holwood about 1943. During February 1946, a hogget strayed on to Venn Farm, East Allington, forty five miles from Molenick and Holwood. I advertised this sheep, seven people came to inspect it, no one claimed it. We sold this sheep on the following June sixth, it fetched twelve pounds. A couple of years later a Mrs Hudson from Higher Heathfield, East Allington about a mile from Venn Farm wrote an article which was published in the Farmer and Stockbreeder about a flock of sheep that had been agisted on her farm during the early part of 1946, a quarter of which had strayed, and never been recovered. It appeared from this that it was more than likely the sheep that had strayed on to Venn Farm came from her agisted sheep. Enquiries revealed that the agisted sheep had been the property of Mr William Tippet who was living somewhere in Cornwall, I knew not where. Perhaps fifty miles away. I never met him again to exchange thanks: me to thank him for indirectly paying for the oats he bought and, he to thank me for mending his car tyre. What I missed most when I moved from Cornwall to Devon was being affectionately addressed as John, Jack or Jan. Holwood Farm enters the highway at right angles. One Callington Sheep Fair day, William Tippet was driving his Austin Seven car to the Fair with his wife in the passenger seat and his shepherd Ed Doney in the back seat, and Callington could be reached by turning right or by turning left, on entering the highway.

If one turned right it took them to Callington via Clapper Bridge Road, via the long steep New Down Hill and Amy Tree. If one turned left it took them to Callington via St Ive. On this occasion when Mr William Tippet entered the highway he drove straight across the road and crashed into the far hedge tipping Ed Doney heavily on his head between himself and his wife in the front seat. After they had sorted themselves out and recovered their speech, Bill's wife said, 'Will, whatever were you thinking about?' He sat up straight and told her, 'I 'main', an' I 'main', I was thinking which way I should go.' She said, 'And which way should we go?' Bill said, 'I 'main', an' I 'main' I'm still wondering about it.'

Mr William Tippet was such a mean man, but very clever in his business dealings. He claimed that he could recognise and remember every sheep he had owned. One autumn, he purchased a lorry load of Black Welsh Mountain ewes. He counted them into one of his fields from a lorry one evening. The next morning they had all strayed from the field and disappeared, but, the following spring, he took a lorry and picked up every one of them. They were spread over five parishes. This confirmed what I had always suspected that he was a crafty ol' so and so.

In about 1933 Hedley and I accompanied by our recently retired farming Uncle Sam, proceeded from Molenick Homestead early one afternoon with a shaft horse attached to a hay wagon and a chain horse to a field facing Luccombe and Blunts known as North Hill, in the centre of which stood a twenty five ton rick of hay.

The field sloped somewhat, the rick stood lengthways with the slope. The wagon was stationed at the bottom end of the rick, the wagon was levelled by lowering the wagon's top wheels. A hay knife was used to cut the portion of the rick required. With the wagon and horses in place Hedley forked the hay to me on the wagon where I built the load. When the hay covered the wagon lades Uncle Sam threw the ropes up to me on the wagon to signal that he considered the load was high enough. Hedley nor I spoke, I just threw the wagon ropes back onto the ground again. Sam said, 'All right, carry on.' We carried on, possibly for devilment, we built a massive load as high and as square as a castle. We duly roped the load down. I took the shaft horse by the head, and controlled the chain horse by rein. The horses moved gently out. I heard someone from behind the load shout 'She's going over.' From the corner of my eye I could see that they were right. I swung the horses heads up the field, the load went over but the shaft horse remained on its feet. We untied the wagon ropes. We attached the chains of the chain horse to the wagon's bottom wheels to haul the wagon out. It took the remainder of that afternoon and the whole of the following morning to reload the hay, to make three wagon loads to clear the hay away. Eleven people saw this happen from Luccombe and several more watched the mishap from Blunts. This was in the so called good old days before the arrival of the tractor and the baler, when we made our own fun, if it could be described as fun. This would not have happened if Uncle Sam had not thrown up the rope prematurely.

DICK DONEY OF TIDEFORD AT THE WHEEL OF HIS TAXI.
YEAR 1930

Dick suffered a slight speech impediment. His s's sounded sh. When his taxi fares asked Dick where they should sit. Dick always replied 'you can shit where you like so long as yu can shit comfortable. It was for this reason his fares invariably made the special point of asking Dick where they should sit.

Dick's taxi was usually well worn. On one occasion when Dick was driving Evelyn's mother, together with other fares, Dick was recounting a few of his most hair raising driving experiences, when Dick suddenly shouted 'and now me shteering wheel hash come off' and there was Dick struggling to fix the wheel back on the steering column.

Between 2 and 6 a.m. on Boxing Day 1927, a severe blizzard struck the South West of England. Poor old Dick's taxi became stuck in the snowdrift on Amy Down. When, a couple of weeks later Dick went back to fetch his taxi, everything removable was missing, including the Bosh magneto.

It was about 1930 that Dick said to me, 'I was driving back from Landrake late last night in heavy rain, there was a man shitting in a stream of water in the gutter half way down Morvah Hill. I stopped the car and what do you think the man was doing,' I said, 'I would guess the man was trying to cover himself with a sheet of galvanised iron to keep himself dry,' Dick said, 'He wash trying to light hish pipe with a glow-worm.' I said, 'Never Mr Doney.' Dick said, 'He wash, that wash what he wash doing.'

A heavy fall of snow fell in late May 1937 which badly singed the potato tops.

Commencing on January 19th 1947 a severe blizzard buried many sheep and completely isolated Venn Farm for six weeks.

1921; 1976; and 1989 were very dry summers. 1889 was a very wet summer, when many thousands of sheep died from caud (liver fluke). 1890 was a dry summer followed by a very mild winter.

The great blizzard of 1891 commenced on March 9th. Snow remained in fields facing North until July.

ALBERT POUND

Albert Pound farmed Tilland Farm during 1930's. Tilland Farm joined Molenick Farm for a short distance.

Albert ran a Jersey cow with his South Devon cows. This Jersey cow gave birth to a heifer calf sired by a South Devon bull.

This heifer calf contracted a bowel infection which brought the calf to death's door. When hope of recovery had appeared to vanish, Albert said to his young son George, the calf is yours if you can bring it around.

The boy persevered with the calf, the calf recovered. When Albert realised the calf

Dick Doney and one of his celebrated Taxis "Sitting" at the wheel

Photo taken 1930.
Charabanc named The Tideford Belle. She was converted from the chassis of a First World War army
transport relic by Dick Haddy (brother of my Uncle Cyril Haddy).
I recall taking one trip in the Belle. The Belle collected eighteen punctures on one of her trips.
I also recall a taxi driven by Dick Haddy collecting seven punctures on a Sunday school trip to Newquay

Left to right: Elizabeth (nee Maddever) holding Monica, Leonard, Gordon and Herbert Greet before Leone was born

would survive, he told the boy to sell it. Albert took the calf to Saltash Market. I bought the calf for 27 shillings. The calf duly developed into a fine square cow, with a fine square udder, superior in shape and in milking ability to the South Devon breed. Albert tried to buy the cow back on several occasions.

The cow's first three calves were heifers which we bred from. These four cows were in the 1941 stock sale.

MISS KATHLEEN (KAYE) MADDEVER

A noteworthy pupil of Launceston Road Council School Callington, when and where May and I attended was Kathleen Maddever.

Kathleen and May sat and passed their eleven plus exams at about the same time, which entitled them to a free education at the Grammar School in Saltash Road Callington.

Kathleen later sat and passed a dairy scholarship which entitled her to further education at Cannington Farm Institute in Somerset.

From these beginnings Kathleen became the greatest living authority on farmhouse Cheddar cheese making.

114

Realizing in their own words thta Kaye Maddever possessed the knowledge that ought to be permanently recorded, the Milk Marketing Board had the good sense to publish a book of her writings and called it 'The Farmhouse Cheesemakers Manual'. It is a fascinating mixture of history, personal recollections, technical information and practical advice.

It has become known as the cheddar cheesemakers bible, it speaks to all those who need the incentive as well as the scientific understanding of cheesemaking generally, and also sheds interesting light on all food manufacturing processes. There are passages and pictures of white bonnetted school children kneading and churning dairy products during the 1930's using ancient equipment right through to the large scale modern stainless machinery of the remaining farmhouse cheesemaking elite in the county today.

The history of good technology reflected in her description of how the early farmhouse pioneers, working with none of the tools of science, attempted to regularise the skills they had acquired by chance and by experience, passing them on to others, a far cry from today's technical terminology and understanding of electronic control and sophisticated machinery.

So effective and repeatable were the methods involved and employed there is no doubt that the work of Kaye and her colleagues turned Cheddar cheese making from a haphazard cottage occupation into a controllable industrial process on a world wide scale.

Kathleen, originally nicknamed Kitty, now more generally known as Kaye has been honoured with the OBE for her personality and for her considerable contribution to the dairy industry. After fifteen years of retirement she is often heard on the radio. She is also an active vice-presidant of the Royal Bath and West Agricultural Show Society, there is probably no living farmhouse cheesemaker in Somerset who has not benefitted from her advice and friendship. When Kaye and her sister Christine drove their pony and jingle to school from their home at Lanhargy they stabled their pony at the Temperence Hotel stables in Pipe Well Street where May and I stabled our pony and jingle when we drove to school from Trewashford, which was in the opposite direction from Lanhargy.

Speaking to Kathleen over the phone recently, I asked her what had happened to the golden locks? She said 'Ah, time has taken its toll, they have been superseded along with many other things that have been superseded during our lifetimes.' Kathleen's brother Ewert and sister Gwen moved from Lanhargy to Castlewick Farm near Callington during the early nineteen twenties. My mother's brother Herbert married Elizabeth Maddever, a not too distant cousin of Kathleen.

CHAPTER 7

Killing to Survive

1944 – 1955

The business of farming is diverse and complex. Probably no other business concern is subjected to the stress, the impelling, or the constraining forces of weather, disease, predators, effort, energy, nature or the ever-changing whims of the consuming public.

Over the weather, no one has any control. One can only accept a presented opportunity set to make the best use of whatever weather conditions prevail at a given time. Over disease, the farmer has to wage a constant battle. Whether he is concerned with producing animals or cultivating plants, success or failure will depend on his ability to win. The most prudent and the cheapest way to win this battle is to breed animals, and to manage the cultivated crops in such a way as to prevent disease.

This generation with its high-powered tractors, its large cultivators, its modern high-cost, oil-based pesticides, fungicides, and herbicides, has frequently abandoned our forefathers' seven years crop rotation system to replace it with a system of plant monoculture — the growing of the same cereal species in the same ground year after year. Monoculture propagates disease at speed for a while in these conditions, until the cereal or plant species comes to terms with some diseases by building up a partial natural resistance. While the health of the cereal species will improve, the cereal species will not produce yields to equal those of the same cereal species grown in our forefathers' seven years crop rotation system. The common sense approach must surely be to rotate crops, using disease break crops every other year to obtain and to maintain maximum crop yields, both from the basic crop and from the break crop. Farming is both an art and a science, only those who can successfully blend the two will be able to fully exploit the two to obtain maximum yields.

Predators have at times to be dealt with, depending on the degree of damage they inflict, whether we like it or not, whether the predators are from a protected species or not. Farmers and farming are increasingly coming under the surveillance of the various nature and wildlife protection societies and groups, which up to a point is reasonable and acceptable, especially so when agriculture is in a buoyant affluent state, when a limited amount of damage and destruction created by protected species

117

is bearable. However, when finances once more become tight in agriculture, protection laws or no protection laws, farmers will have no choice but to become as ruthless with the protected species as the protected species are ruthless with the farmer.

The tractor, the four, five or six furrow plough, a seed bed produced by just one pass of a powered rotary cultivator, the combined fertiliser and seed drill, heavier yielding varieties of autumn and spring sown wheat and barley, and disease controlled by expensive sprays, together with the modern combine harvester, have revolutionised the growing of cereals. During the period between the two Great Wars a 1¼ ton an acre yield from wheat and barley was a top yield. In 1985 a 2½ ton an acre yield for barley, and a 3 ton an acre yield for wheat, in corn-growing areas is regarded only as a moderate yield. The plant breeders, the spray producers, heavier applications of nitrogen and improved husbandry have each contributed to more than doubling the yields of cereals.

Over the years farming has changed from mixed farming with the random keeping of a few milking cows, beef animals, sheep, pigs, and fowls, mainly fed from home-grown grass, hay and cereals to the specialised production of just a few of the commodities, whether it be milk, beef, mutton, pigs, eggs, capons, cereals, potatoes, sugar beet, oil seed rape, peas or whatever. The cost of production is carefully monitored, and the return from each product is carefully analysed and appraised.

The Dairy Shorthorn, once the main milk-producing breed of cattle, has since the last war been replaced by what has become known as the British Friesian, a large-framed animal producing large quantities of milk. The large-framed strains of this black and white breed will produce quality beef progeny when crossed with a quality beef bull.

Unfortunately producers with milk on their brains have imported Holstein cattle from Canada, a breed similar in colour and in style to the British Friesian which produces heavier milk yields but also possesses inferior beefing qualities. While these Holstein cattle might further increase an already oversupplied milk commodity, the beef producer will lose more than the Holstein milk producer will gain. Among the main breeds of cattle in this country now producing milk are the British Friesian, the Ayrshire, the Guernsey and the Jersey. Among the beef breeds of cattle in this country are Aberdeen Angus, Beef Shorthorn, Belgian Blue, Blonde d'Aquitaine, Charolais, Devon, Galloway, Golbieh, Hereford, Highland, Limousin, Lincoln Red Shorthorn, Luing, Murray Grey, Romagnola, Salers, Semmintal, South Devon, Sussex and Welsh Blacks. Among Britain's rare breeds are the Kerry, Red Poll, Long Horn, White Cattle and Blue Albion.

Time was when the high butterfat producing breeds such as the Guernsey, Jersey, Ayrshire and possibly the South Devon each kept the odd British Friesian cow in the herd to use its milk to rinse out the milking pails and the milking utensils. By the year 1985, through selective breeding, the butterfat content of the British

Friesian cows' milk had improved to the extent when the British Friesian breed dominated milk production. By comparison few Dairy Shorthorn, Ayrshire, Guernsey and Jersey herds now exist.

The value of the British Friesian calf when it has been sired by a good beef bull has favoured the British Friesian breed. Local pure beef breeds such as the Beef Shorthorn, the Lincoln Red Shorthorn, the North Devon, and the Sussex have been superseded by the heavy carcase, lean meat producing mainly Continental breeds such as the Belgian Blue, the Blonde d'Aquitaine, the Charolais, the Limousin, the Semmintal and a few others.

Quality meat, the meat with the best flavour, is still produced from British breeds, the Aberdeen Angus being considered the very best, followed by the South Devon, followed again by the Hereford and possibly the Sussex, even the Beef Shorthorn and the Lincoln Red Shorthorn. Strains of bigger-framed Herefords are being imported to increase the size of the Hereford to enable it to compete with the Continental breeds. Before the last war, almost every butcher was shouting for the farmer to produce smaller beef cattle to provide for small joints, and butchers paid high premiums for small fat cattle. The fashion has changed since the arrival of the large Continental breeds. Amazingly butchers have discovered smaller knives which enable them to cut smaller joints from bigger carcases. It was unfortunate these small knives were not available during the 1930's.

The Limousin bull is now crossed with the South Devon cows to improve the conformation of the South Devon breed. While in my younger days the South Devon breed was not uniform in appearance there were some good beef strains of South Devon, that is until its breed society tried to turn the breed into a dual purpose breed — when A.I. was first introduced in 1944 for milk and beef and it fell badly between the two stools.

During my earlier days British farmers were acclaimed as the premier stockbreeders and stockmasters of the world.

Times must have changed if the recent importations of the many new breeds are anything to go by.

During the 1930's when Plate maize, French wheat, and Russian barley could be purchased at prices between £4 and £5 a ton, we fattened cattle at grass supplemented with one feed of rolled cereals each day. During one period there were about 20 cattle running in the fields in front of Kilquite House which were being fed rolled cereals in a wooden manger extending the length of the shed in the corner of one of these fields. One morning we had sorted out some sheep which were to be collected by a cattle lorry to be transported to Saltash cattle market for sale in the afternoon. I thought I had time to rush over to feed these 20 cattle with rolled cereals before the arrival of the cattle lorry. I placed the rolled cereals in the manger and I called the cattle which were making for the shed. I observed which were the first to arrive, the rest were following behind in a hurry. I foolishly did not wait to see how many reached the manger before I rushed away. Albert Courts, crossing these fields the following day, came across a bullock in the corner of the field which was in a sitting position completely oblivious of Albert's presence.

As soon as Albert had told me of his discovery, I realised what had happened. I jumped on my motor bike and visited the animal, it was the first that had entered the shed the previous day. It had obviously eaten too many cereals. I should have seen them all at the trough feeding before I left them the previous day. I returned home and 'phoned Mr Fernly Rogers at Landrake, a wholesale butcher. I told him the story, he said 'What about anthrax?' I said 'I know the animal is down through eating too many cereals.' He said 'I will be able to tell if it is anthrax when I bleed it. I will come right out.' I 'phoned around for a cattle lorry and Mr Arthur Snowden answered the call. I arranged for William Symons to be at the scene with two horses to drag the carcase to the road.

Mr Rogers arrived. The animal was apparently dead, but it bled freely. The horses dragged the carcase to the Tilland end of the field, and we conveyed it to Mr Rogers' slaughter house. When the animal was dressed it was found to be bung full of corn which had swollen and created a stoppage in the intestines. It was a first class carcase which qualified for the five shillings a hundredweight premium which the Government had been paying farmer producers at the time. This animal realised £24, this was enough money to pay one man's wages of thirty-two shillings a week for fifteen weeks of forty eight hours each.

The same weight animal would realise £600 at today's prices which is enough to pay one man's wages at £3 an hour for five weeks of forty hours each, or two hundred hours of work during 1985 compared with seven hundred and twenty hours work during the 1930's.

I have, on many occasions, got out of bed between 2 and 3 a.m. to keep an eye on a cow calving, a sow farrowing, a mare foaling, or a ewe lambing.

On one such visit to a cow at Molenick she was in the act of calving. While the calf was presented correctly she needed help to deliver it, or perhaps more correctly, because I had taken the trouble to get out of bed and did not want to hang around in the cold night air I had decided that I would help her, when perhaps I should have gone back to bed. Nature usually has its own way of solving its problems even if in the process it causes more pain. If we give a mother sufficient time her pushing will in time produce more room for the offspring to come through, so there are times when we should leave the mother and nature to get on with the job by themselves when all else is in order. On the other hand, if we leave them alone too long the mother can become exhausted, or the offspring might succumb, so it is a question of accurate timing.

Maybe on this occasion I was an hour too soon with help, but I wanted to get back to bed. The calf was in really good condition, it had probably gone over its normal time. All went well until the delivery reached the pins (hips) where it became stuck.

The house was small which prevented me from using my full strength, our combined strengths were not sufficient to move it and there was no help within half a mile. The pressure from the cow while the calf was stuck in that position slowly forced the calf's intestines through its navel.

Eventually together we got the calf away. I put its intestines back and held them there. All I needed was someone there to fetch some stitching material. I only had the hurricane lantern for light, what was I to do? I know now what I should have done, I should have taken off my shirt and bound it tightly around the middle of the calf. Eventually I became bored. I decided to make a dash and fetch some stitching material from the house, across the orchard, along the path where my father carried the ten shilling note, along the drive, across the cobbled yard and into the house. Alas, by the time I got back to the calf, so much of its entrails were out that I could not replace them on my own. It was very disappointing for I had to put the calf down.

On one occasion when I was alone on the farm a cow calving out in the field required assistance. I attached pulley blocks to the calf's feet, and attached the other end of the pulley blocks to an iron bar driven into the ground. I pulled the cow around the field until I tethered the cow's head to another stake driven into the ground.

During the mid 1930's our large South Devon bull and a slightly smaller South Devon bull from Cutcrew Farm frequently bellowed at each other across the valley. After milking one summer evening our bull, with the cows, had been put for the night to graze in Meladrim Field. When Cutcrew bull came out on top of the hill across the valley and commenced bellowing at our bull, our bull decided it was about time that he went over to this other bull and shut his trap.

So our bull put its head to the field's road gate, lifted the gate from its hinges, strolled leisurely down the road, put its head to one of Cutcrew Farm's fields gates, lifted this gate from its hinges, and made its way across some fields to where this other bull was still bellowing. People at Tideford Cross had heard this bellowing and had reported it to stone-deaf Granfer Holding, who had been in charge of Cutcrew cows and this bull. He appeared on the scene in time to see these two bulls commence their argument. Granfer Holding was delighted when eventually our bull pushed Cutcrew bull down the hill and into the hedge at the bottom. The two bulls then parted, the Cutcrew bull returned to his harem, while our bull casually retraced his steps to Meladrim Field. The bellowing had stopped. Apparently Cutcrew bull had recently attacked Granfer holding and that was why he was so pleased to see the Cutcrew bull vanquished. Father, Mother, Cordelia and Herbert had witnessed the bull fight from Molenick Farmhouse. I had been working at Kilquite that evening, and Herbert came over in his car to fetch me. We met our bull strolling leisurely up the road on its way to its own field, completely unruffled.

Before 1940 Granfer Holding had retired and a new cowman had taken his place.

121

During the spring of 1940 we grew broccoli in a field known as East Park which adjoins Cutcrew fields. Cutcrew cows had been breaking into this field and this cowman had known it. He also knew that the hedge had not been fenced against these cows, so he turned the cows into another field for the night. The farmer's wife inquired from the cowman what he was doing. The cowman explained but she ordered him to put the cows back and he did. He then came straight to me and told me what had happened. I thanked him and I promised I would not implicate him. I kept an eye on the broccoli field and just after midnight the cows commenced entering. I tried to 'phone Cutcrew but there was no answer. I took a walking stick and walked across the fields to Cutcrew Farmhouse where I banged on the farmhouse door. Bill Dawe, the husband, popped his head out of the window, he said 'Who is it?' I said 'It is me, Bill.' We have got trouble, you had better dress and come down.' When he arrived dressed I said 'Bill, you had better come with me.'

When we reached the broccoli field I asked 'Are those your cows Bill?' He said 'Yes.' I said 'We will drive them out through the road gate, from then on they are yours.' I said 'Bill, these cows are not to enter this field again,' and they didn't.

Bill ran the timber business, his wife ran the farm. Bill was alright, we had been good friends before, and were good friends after. It was Bill who had brought three evacuees to our house for my ageing mother to look after and took one to his house for his comparatively young wife to look after.

The next South Devon bull that we kept after the one that fought Cutcrew bull was grazing with cows in Meladrim Field one day when I went to fetch him. It was unusual, in that the bull was standing alone about a hundred yards from the gate, a considerable distance from the cows. At first it did not concern me, but when I sent the dog to fetch the bull, for the first time in its life it refused. It kept behind me as if cowering, I tried coaxing it, but to no avail. This set me thinking. I looked at the bull, its eyes were fixed on me, its front feet were still, but its hind feet were being moved up and down. I remembered that I had seen this motion before when a steer had charged me and I also recalled the experience of my mother's half-brother William.

Uncle William once entered a field where the bull stood alone. The heifers he had been running with were in another field out of sight. Uncle William had sent his dog after the heifers in the next field when this bull attacked him. The bull tore off almost every shred of clothing from his body, very badly bruising him in the process. When the dog returned it set about the bull, and while the dog attacked the bull Uncle William crawled under the field gate to safety. The dog had saved his life. The villagers collected for and purchased a special collar for this dog which was suitably inscribed.

I decided that caution was the better part of valour. For once I took the easy way out, for once I was yellow. I left the bull where it was.

One must learn to treat bulls, rams and stallions with the utmost respect, never to pet or pamper them or to grant them liberties. It is far more sensible to occasion give them a good cuff with a stout stick to remind them who is the boss. One shou. never enter a field where there is a bull, a stallion, or a boar, without some form of stout defence. A strong four-pronged fork in one's hands commands their greatest respect.

Rams are usually the least dangerous, but rams can hit pretty hard with their heads. They can bruise one very badly, and can break bones. We are rarely bothered with a wicked ram these days, but when we were boys every ram was wicked and would fight you at every opportunity, thanks to Hedley who would tease them until they reacted. During those days we always took a halter to tie them to a gate when we were trimming their feet or docking them out. They never attacked father because he always carried a stick. I remember once when docking out a sheep with shears at Molenick that a ram butted me in the backside unexpectedly and with force while I was kneeling on one knee. It sent me flying. Quite apart from the bruising, a pair of shears in one's hands can be very dangerous.

A man working in a field on one side of a valley observed another man enter a field on the opposite side of the valley in which a flock of sheep grazed, and where a rick of hay stood in the centre. The man on the opposite side of the valley had not moved far into the field before a ram detached itself from the flock to chase him. The man took to his heels and made for the safety of the hay rick. The ram pushed the man hard, they circled the rick at speed. Eventually the ram slowed then stopped. The man had been travelling so fast that he could not prevent himself from overtaking the ram round the corner, while the ram took off after him again in hot pursuit. A boar pig with full tusks can be the most dangerous and I know two men who were very badly ripped by their vicious tusks. While at Venn Farm one of our boar pigs strayed to a field where there were young cattle grazing. The first thing the boar did was to walk up to one of the bullocks and rip its stomach open with one of its tusks. That was another bullock we were forced to put down but, I skinned and dressed this carcase for our own use. Since moving to Venn Farm we lost a cow which had rolled on to its back with its head lying upstream in a slight depression made by a tiny stream in our bottom meadow. Its body had blocked the stream which we had assumed drowned her. Some time later while a vet was on the farm an employee reported a cow on her back with her head lying up the hill in an excavated hollow at the foot of a recently rebuilt earth hedge. The vet, the employee and myself hastened to where the cow lay. I said, 'Let us pull her around.' but the vet said not to move her. He started examining her. We watched her die. A post mortem revealed that she had drowned in her own saliva. The saliva having flooded her lungs. Had the truth been known this may also have caused the death of the first cow. We have since piped the stream underground, and levelled the hedges. The time is fast approaching when we will require the permission of ill-informed misguided urban authorities to do these things. As from May 1922, when father purchased a left-hand drive Ford T one ton lorry, sheep were transported to and from market by road in the lorry. It was not until about 1930 that cattle were transported by lorry. Up until this date these animals were 'walked' to and from market, which was a slow, tedious haul.

On several occasions between 1925 and 1930 I have 'walked' fat cattle, sometimes singly, on my own from Molenick Farm to Saltash Market, a distance of seven miles. I remember on one occasion a single fat steer that I had been 'walking' to Saltash Market becoming fatigued, and wanting to lie down in the road by the time it had reached Latchbrook Farm in the valley, on the old road, which was owned and farmed by Uncle Thomas. I managed to 'walk' it into Latchbrook Farm yard and closed the entrance doors. I went on to Saltash Market where father had preceded me in the jingle. Father said, 'We will get a butcher to visit Latchbrook Farm after the sale with a view to the butcher buying it.' When we arrived at Latchbrook with Mr Jane, a Saltash butcher, and entered the yard, the steer was standing in the far corner staring at us. It was moving its back feet up and down ominously and the steer soon charged while the three of us shot into separate doors. Fortunately, father had remained in the jingle outside the entrance door. I was inside a door nearest the steer, I asked the other two to open a couple of doors at the far end of the yard, with a view to enticing the steer into one of these houses. After the two doors had been opened I moved out into the yard, when the steer charged after me I entered one door, the steer the other. I slipped out to shut and fasten the door behind the steer which had become demented and they shot him there in the morning. The person in the yard was Uncle Tom.

When newly-calved cows were sold at auction, the cow's calf would usually be put into the back of a cart, trap or spring wagon when the cow would follow behind. We have often taken newly-weaned farrows or slip pigs to market in a cart, a trap or a spring wagon. The pigs were often purchased by someone living a few miles from the market in the opposite direction from your own home and the vendor was expected to deliver the pigs, sometimes sold for as little as eight shillings each. There were cattle drovers in every market town who hired themselves out to drive cattle to and from the markets. The last family of drovers that I can recall were the Nettles of Callington.

As a boy my father was often sent by his father, and by neighbouring farmers, to call the vet for difficult calving cases, there having been no 'phones at that time. The vets would always ask Father whether it was a cow or a first calf heifer which required attention. If it was a cow the vet would come immediately. If it was a first calf heifer the vet would say 'I will be along as soon as I can,' which meant that he was intentionally giving the heifer time to prepare for calving.

The transportation of animals for breeding and for finishing is unavoidable. The business of transporting live animals long distances before slaughter to satisfy some religious ritual, or to make an extra buck, is obscenely cruel and evil and should not be permitted even if this results in the bankruptcy of the entire farming community. It should be stated here that it is the trade which moves the animals long distances, not the farmers, but it sometimes affects the financial returns of farmers. If animals are transported with full stomachs it will frequently cause the death of the animals even when being transported only short distances. For an animal to travel in comfort its stomach must be empty. It costs at least twice as much to transport live animals over a given distance as it costs to transport animal carcases, possibly four times as much. It is neither prudent nor necessary to transport live animals beyond the next county to a place of slaughter. Compassion for the animals should decree that no animals going for slaughter should travel beyond the next county.

Farmers quite literally have to kill to survive. Among the first things working farmers' sons are taught is to kill. Killing includes all manner and type of disease, weed, pest, predators.

While the sheltered cosseted urban dweller is deeply shaken when confronted with death, death is witnessed almost daily on the farm. This might be considered by them to inspire farmer's sons to become callous and insensitive to pain and to suffering, this is not necessarily so. It will enable farmers' sons to understand nature and to apply logic to a specific circumstance, compared to the often illogical conclusions and opinions expressed by the sheltered, inexperienced and often biased urban dweller. At the present time the urban dweller is deeply concerned for the welfare of wildlife, and rightly so, but they often have not sufficient experience of nature to make an unbiased, rational assessment, and for this reason will too often leap at the wrong conclusions. The editors of our current daily and weekly newspapers are also too inexperienced to be in a position to make a sensible assessment of what is logical in a farming business. For example, take the following letter from Mr John Charlesworth, Poundsgate, near Newton Abbot, Devon, which appeared under the heading, 'letters' in the local paper Plymouth dated 9.2.1986 and which also appeared in another local paper: SAVE THE BADGERS. 'A 'phone call, a dying badger had been found in the road. The injuries described were unmistakably the result of vicious badger-baiting. The torn flesh around the neck where the cruel chain had held while the dogs savaged its hindquarters. But Brock had found peace at last in Mother Nature's cool, sweet earth never more to be tormented by the creature homo sapiens that crawled from the primeval slime to become the species that walks erect, made in the image of God, who has a soul and is an abomination in the universe. Ninety nine per cent of the people in this country are revolted at this constant cruelty by the one per cent. Everybody should be on his or her guard and report any clue (however trivial) to the police. Our coppers would love to get their hands on these sub-humans. We should be grateful for the Tony Edens and Tony Kerrs of the world, champions in a vast-growing army of people dedicated to stop this senseless cruelty.

Help them before Mother Nature throws us all in the abyss to eternity, for if

Nostradamus is right this fitting end to our species is not too far away.

Signed John Charlesworth.'

Eighteen months before this happening three badgers lay dead on the roads which intersect this farm, all of which had been run over and killed by cars, perhaps driven over deliberately by the drivers.

I have been closely associated with badgers all my life. Badgers are the noblest of creatures, we admire them immensely, we have supported their existence. For every badger that existed in this area when we came to this farm 48 years ago, there are at present 50.

No one around here has used dogs to dig out badgers for a very long while. Not withstanding this, and contrary to what we are frequently being told, the most humane way of controlling the badger population when necessary is to dig them out, using dogs, and to dispatch them humanely — but spare some compassion for the dog. During a lifetime's experience I have never once witnessed a badger-baiting session taking place, or suspected a single case of badger-baiting having taken place.

The placing of a chain around its neck to tether the badger is a completely new figment of fantasy. It is simply not feasible, the badger's neck is as large as the badger's head. In the eyes of a moderately logical thinking man, the finding of an injured dying badger lying on the road would suggest the badger had been struck by a car. A reasonably logical thinking man would not leap to the extremely unlikely conclusions of Mr John Charlesworth. He appears to have permitted his superior imagination and education to have overtaken him. Almost every week we are fed a similar story of alleged brutal badger baiting in these two papers. It gives these printed issues the appearance of being animal lovers, waging war against human cruelty to animals. This propaganda is lapped up and relished by the innocently unsuspecting gullible urban dweller. It certainly encourages the sales of newspapers, but it would be refreshing to hear the other side occasionally. I very much doubt whether these alleged badger baiting sessions in whatever form they exist to anything like the extent these two newspapers claim, and would have us believe. These same papers print one side only of this contention. I have written letters to both of these editorials on several occasions putting forward other facets of their contentions, but my letters have never been published. Have these two newspapers been afraid to publish the other side? Are they more concerned with playing to the gallery than with the truth and preying on the sympathy of their readers in the hope of selling more papers? It is doubtful if these two newspapers are actually concerned with the suffering of animals at all. I respectfully asked the British Broadcasting Company if the badger-baiting sessions shown on our screens are factual and authentic. It seemed to me as an observant viewer that the animal that the terriers were attacking was already a dead animal. I understand that the B.B.C. has been requested to name the time and the place where this alleged badger baiting session has taken place but the B.B.C. refused to disclose this information.

Working farmers' sons, and not infrequently farmers' daughters, are brought face to face at an early age with the realities of life, of living, with the pleasant and the not so pleasant experiences of this world. They are forced to conclude that where there is life there is suffering. Where there is birth, there is death. In many cases death can be a welcome relief from pain. A morbid subject, which many people would wish to avoid, but which farming people are not able to avoid as they are compelled as part of their livelihood to witness every day of their lives.

Nature itself, uncompromising and wonderful as it is, creates most of the suffering among living creatures throughout the Universe, but this fact should not create a licence for humans to be cruel. The four wonderful seasons of the year that we worship can be the cause of major stress to wildlife. When extreme climatic conditions are encountered, much wildlife perishes from hypothermia, starvation or thirst. The perils of Arctic conditions cause starvation and thirst as do the extreme arid conditions. Living so close to nature and to the four seasons farming families witness many nasty, unavoidable scenes, when animal predators capture and cruelly tear defenceless creatures apart in their quest for food and their own survival. Not unnaturally, the sympathy of the farmer's children leaps to the aid of the silent, suffering, defenceless, innocent creatures, the victims of the animal predator in contrast to the average misguided townspeople who sometimes even gloat over the predator's victory. The farmer, the arch predator, will destroy as humanely as he knows how, the enemies that would kill the animals in his care. This is the conflict that farmers face. Many people want to protect the predators. There has been produced a mass of legislation to protect the lives and to maintain the survival of many predatorspecies. At the shameful expense of the innocent defenceless lives of the lesser, weaker species who suffer silently without the assistance of a single prick of conscience from the predator worshippers.

When badgers become too numerous the simplest and possibly the most humane method for putting them and fox cubs to sleep is by using tractor exhaust fumes. Badgers and fox cubs spend the daytime in holes. If a few partly filled polythene bags were provided to block the holes the operation would be difficult to detect.

Farmers are now liable to a fine of up to two thousand pounds for even disturbing a badger's set, in spite of the fact that badgers destroy more than three hundred pounds worth of corn on our farm every year. Also the fact that badgers are reasonably believed to reinfect cattle worth one thousand pounds each. The new legislation seems to contradict the issue of The Ministry having spent many millions of tax payers' money eradicating tuberculosis from bovine animals. We are living in a crazy world.

NATURE SEEKING THE TRUTH

The badger is a noble creature, far nobler than the normal human creature.

Through the facts of life, and the laws of nature, there is no room on this planet for every badger that could be conceived, for every human that could be conceived, or for every member of any species of animal, or any species of plant that could be conceived or produced.

When there is room it invariably is at the expense of the lives of many members of other species of living creature. If God is nature, if nature is God, if the laws of nature are God's laws, then these laws are in direct conflict with the commandment 'Thou shall not kill', and in direct conflict with the teaching of Jesus.

If God is nature, God must also be Lord of the jungle, where the strongest prey upon the weakest, where the strong survive, where the weak go to the wall. Without God showing the slightest compassion, and Lord of all natural disasters, droughts, frosts, blizzards, earthquakes, pestilence, hurricanes, tornados, and floods, as well as Lord of the joyous springtime when songbirds mate, and when the buds and the leaves appear on the trees. The Lord which farmers' boys can walk side by side, hand in hand, and the Lord which farmers' boys often have no option but to fight. From the evidence available, God and Jesus possess nothing whatever in common, they are as far removed from each other as are the poles, they are as unlike as darkness and light, their principles are in direct conflict, they each foster, support and promote opposing principles, standards and influences.

With nature and heredity being what it is, it appears alien, unnatural and doubtful — as are so many claims made by Christians — that this supernatural God is the father of Jesus, in the eyes of this simple very ordinary country being.

Over the centuries Christian doctrines have been founded on guilt, on fear and on punishment for the wrongdoer. Over the centuries organised Christianity has created, perfected, perpetrated and perpetuated the most subtle and deceitful confidence trick ever employed by man, to hoodwink trusting unsuspecting gullible, incapable of thinking for themselves members of the human race for no other purpose than to feather their own financial nests.

That the world is in desperate need of leadership in truthfulness, honesty, humility, selflessness, morality, and in compassion, is fully accepted and not in dispute. The question is, can these desirable qualities be achieved if the concept of Christianity is founded upon deceit rather than upon truth. While nature might not be able to teach humans how to arrange words to explain God's involvement with mankind, nature can teach humans all that can possibly be known about God and God's relationship with mankind will permit itself to be taught. It is about time Christians stopped fantasising. It is time Christians stopped playing little earthly Gods and admitted that in spite of all the preaching, in spite of all the bickering, the barbarism, the bloodshed, the strife and the anguish which in the past has bedevilled the Christian world, since the coming of Jesus, all that can truthfully be said about life is that life on this earth is as precious to individual members of the animal kingdom as it is to individual members of the human kingdom and probably twice as deserving.

In the light of modern experience of nature, it is expecting a lot to expect anyone to believe that Jesus was fathered by a super-natural being. It is also about time Christians came clean and admitted that the origin of life on this earth is still a complete mystery, that no one knows from whence life cometh or whither life goeth, and that it is more practical to follow and to worhip the life and the example of Jesus that it is to worship a super-natural illusion.

The conservation of wildlife especially when it concerns animal predators is an emotive subject.

It is not generally appreciated that during the lifetime of the average animal predator it kills and consumes a thousand defenceless victims.

Is the life of an animal predator more important or more precious than the lives of its thousand defenceless victims. Reproduction of the human predator is controlled by contraception, induced abortion, accidents, by diseases contracted by a physically weaker human species, whose roaming nature exposes them to increased infection, by strife between human races, between religious factions within human races, and between individual humans. If reproduction among animal predator species continues unchecked, it will only be a matter of time before animal predator species will run out of defenceless victims to keep them alive, and will turn on members of other predator species to maintain its survival.

My Uncle John of Bealbury was for many years, by permission of the owner of the Pentille Estates, St Mellion and by permission of the tenants of the estate, the master of three hare coursing meetings each year, one held in December, one in January, and one in February until 1934, on and around Viverdon, and Westcott Farms, meeting by Amy Tree. When two greyhounds were released after one hare, most of the hares got away, but a few were caught. We were raised in these surroundings, it appeared the natural way of weeding out the weak to maintain the survival of the species. We had not seen cruelty involved when controlling their numbers in this way, until these misguided, busybodies commenced raising their voices. No doubt, from their angle this is cruel, but, we can assure them the operation was absolutely necessary.

The hares themselves were not predators or killers, neither are deer which are hunted by hounds. We, eventually, came around to agreeing with these interfering busybodies. We are now ready to accept their views, that, at the present time, there are so many other pleasant ways available for passing our time, that we should no longer need to chase innocent hares or innocent deer merely for fun.

For some unexplained reason since 1934, hares seem to have disappeared from Viverdon, maybe now that hares are not being preserved for sport no one is prepared or willing to preserve them just to look at, or to eat their crops. There are no longer any hares to course.

As a family we have never been ardent supporters of hunting. Following hounds is a waste of time. You won't see many successful farmers following hounds at every

Amy Tree
A hare coursing meeting December 1922
Uncle John holding a saddle which had been presented to him by followers.
Mr Runnals and Mr Joe Snell with slips.
Brother Hedley, aged 16 years two months, can be seen holding hare just to Uncle John's right. Our father's
T.
Ford ton lorry which William drove can be seen by the tree on the right of the picture.

meet unless they possess an independent income. While I enjoy the music of the hounds while running, I could never afford the time to follow them, or to stand and stare. Our children have reared a couple of hound pups for the local harrier pack, and the pack hunt over our land. That is the extent of our involvement with hunting. As far as we are concerned hunting can be stopped from tomorrow. It has been customary for us to keep a terrier dog to kill rats and to mark rabbits to ground when ferreting.

Not long after foxes were introduced into the area they commenced killing newly-born lambs. Ralph Tall of Ranscombe Farm 'phoned me one morning and said 'There is a fox in the field where our ewes our lambing, will you bring down your terrier.' Michael and I went down with our terrier and a Devon shovel. The terrier marked the fox in a single hole in the field bank. A spade's depth from the top of the bank we came upon the vixen, with cubs. Michael said he was going to rear one of the cubs. I said 'How do you propose doing that?' He said 'With a spoon.' I said 'Put it with the litter of pups the collie bitch is rearing in the barn,' which he did. We dispatched the remaining cubs.

When the fox cub was taken outside the barn, after it had been with her puppies for a couple of days the collie bitch would carry it back by its neck to her own puppies. The fox cub and the collie pups matured together. We sold the collie pups except two. As time passed, the fox cub became semi-wild and commenced luring the collie pups away from the farm.

I said to Michael 'If you don't put the fox cub down, it will start taking our neighbours' domestic fowls during the daytime and this will cause friction.' One day Michael saw the fox cub lead the pups in the direction of the valley. He fetched his gun and followed them almost a mile down the valley before he was able to shoot the fox cub.

There were unwelcome consequences attached to rearing this fox cub. Not long after the cub had been brought to the barn we commenced collecting fleas. These fleas multiplied in numbers until they reached epidemic proportions. It was a couple of years before they were completely annihilated.

When we came to this farm 41 years ago, there was scarcely a badger, fox, mink, or a grey squirrel to be found anywhere in this area. The steel gins used for catching wild rabbits saw to that. Magpies and crows abounded. These magpies and crows ate many of the hens' eggs, and killed baby chicks of the geese, turkey, duck and laying hen species, if given the slightest opportunity. I placed strychnine in rats and nailed the rats to the old stumps of ash pots which grew on the field hedges. Only a sow, a hungry hound, or the occasional hungry cat amongst domesticated animals will eat a dead rat. This killed every magpie that came on to the farm, and most of the crows.

We kept 500 laying hens on free range without shutting them up at night without losing a single hen from badgers or foxes, from the time that we came to this farm until the steel rabbit gin was outlawed, until the rabbit had been killed off by myxomatosis, until the hunting people had introduced numerous fox cubs. At the time that we kept the 500 laying hens on free range, we also reared their replacements, plus up to 90 goslings a year, several turkeys, ducks, chicken for table, and guinea fowl. At the present time there is not a single domestic fowl kept on the farm, a domestic fowl would not survive 24 hours on free range because of predators. When foxes made their first appearance in this area, we had on one occasion retired for the night when Evelyn woke me and said 'I can hear a sound like bones being cracked or broken.' We crept out of bed and listened from the bedroom window, which you always left open. The farmhouse was high, the garden beneath the bedroom window was surrounded by a stone wall while the ground beyond the garden dropped several feet. The previous day a lorry load of stone aggregate had been tipped against this stone wall, on which grew a shrub and in which a couple of laying hens roosted.

The bone-cracking noise turned out to be a fox trying to walk up to the top of this heap of aggregate to take one of the laying hens. Eventually the fox managed to seize one of the hens which commenced squalling and it carried the hen out into the field beyond the garden. I crept downstairs to fetch a gun and a cartridge, but by the time I arrived back at the window the fox had moved out of sight. The moon was setting.

We returned to bed. Some hours later, after the moon had set and there was complete darkness, we heard a fox attempting to mount the heap of aggregate to reach the second laying hen roosting in the shrub, almost underneath the bedroom window. We got out of bed again. I picked up the gun that had been left lying on the window sill and noticed that the night had become completely dark. The fox grabbed the hen, the hen commenced to squeal. I listened carefully to the sound of the crying hen and pointed the gun in the direction of the sound. When I considered the fox had emerged from the shelter of the garden wall I pulled the trigger of the gun. The silence of the night was suddenly shattered. The report from the 12 bore gun echoed and re-echoed down the valley and the night was filled with the sound of turkeys gobbling, geese babbling and snipes shrieking. I dressed and visited a sow that was farrowing, she had just given birth to what I had expected was the first farrow. I went to discover if I had killed the fox, I saw nothing.

First thing in the morning I revisited the sow but there were no more farrows, just the one. Evelyn joined me and together we visited the scene of the previous night's fox shoot. The fox was there dead, it was a vixen. There was no sign of the hen. The fox had probably died of fright. That fox was one of the 400 adult foxes we killed on Venn Farm during four years.

Ninety-three cubs and adult foxes were killed on our neighbour's farms between one Easter and the following Whitsun one year in addition to the 400 killed on Venn Farm which possessed no waste land to harbour foxes. Therefore the 400 killed had been journeying through.

Many years ago we had noticed from their footprints in the snow that the odd fox travelled from corn rick to corn rick as if it was looking for food, which we had assumed was a rat. So, when the fox population exploded in this part of South Devon we baited rats with poison, and placed them by the corn ricks in the fields. When the combine harvester replaced the corn rick, we placed the baited rats in fox runs on the tops of hedges.

An easy way for drawing and destroying foxes is to exploit the heap of fresh stable manure while it is fermenting and just bury dead cats, domestic or wild fowl, or carrion of any description in the centre of this steaming heap. The wind will carry the scent of the decaying flesh for at least a couple of miles and draw the foxes to the spot. Place poisoned rats around the heap of stable manure. As the rats disappear replace these with more poisoned rats. Addled eggs placed in the heating heap of stable manure will draw a fox three miles, a cow's placenta will draw a fox the same distance.

Poisoning predators and vermin is probably the cruellest method of controlling their numbers. As the more humane methods of controlling predator and vermin numbers are being eroded through Government legislation introduced to appease few well meaning, but misguided, warped, cranky, interfering busybodies, poisoning of predators and vermin can be undertaken without anyone knowing and without the risk of prosecution. For while strychnine is now unobtainable there are plenty of poisons freely available on the market which can replace strychnine. Don't blame the farmers for this undesirable and unwelcome trend. The urban dweller's entire food supply depends on controlling the unwelcome predators. It is not yet possible that predator species and vermin species can control their numbers by the use of contraceptives or by induced abortions, as do the human species. During one January I caught nineteen foxes and nine badgers in snares. Three of the badgers were found dead in the snares, three of them were mangy, I put these down. Three badgers were healthy, these I released. No one who is not experienced with handling badgers should ever attempt to release them from the snares. Badgers are immensely strong, they not only bite hard, they will not release their hold for they possess jaws of steel. One of the badgers that we released was very powerful and it put up quite a fight. We, eventually, succeeded in releasing it. After its release we watched it trundle along to a set at the bottom of a thirteen acre field that Michael had planted to oats that spring. During the summer badgers dug several holes and created a large set in the centre of the thirteen acre field of oats. They destroyed more than one acre of oats in that field by rolling and trampling it down, thereby ruining two and a half tons of oats valued at one hundred pounds per ton. One morning during the following winter I was on the way to market when I met Trevor, my second son. He said, 'There is a badger caught in a snare in Gratton field.' I said, 'Take the gun and shoot it.' He hesitated: 'I don't like killing it.' I answered, 'None of us do, but it is too dangerous for you to release it on your own.' Trevor then suggested that he would try to turn it loose. I then told him, 'Then I will go with you.' He collected the necessary wire-cutters and we returned together to the snared animal. The badger lay still while Trevor cut the wire and removed it from its neck. The relieved creature looked up at him as if to say, 'Thank you.' rose up from the snare, shook itself and leisurely ambled away to the set at the bottom of the oat field. I said to Trevor, 'That is the same old rascal that we let loose from the next field.' I wondered then, and have wondered many times since, how many of these badger worshippers would release a creature that had helped to destroy two hundred and fifty pounds worth of food from their garden.

I had spent three trips to hospital totalling more than thirty weeks when the fox population explosion took place. Foxes had been killing dozens of newly-born lambs. Some farmers got together and formed a Fox Destruction Society using beaters and guns. A Mr Owen Steer was appointed secretary. Our family had nothing to do with this society but as soon as it commenced operation, they called on Michael who was fifteen years of age and carried a twelve bore gun, to assist them with his terrier. When I was home between my trips to hospital Mr Ralph Tall of Ranscombe telephoned asking us to bring our terrier down as he had seen a fox among his lambing ewes. Michael and I went down. Mr Owen Steer reported the fact that we had killed a vixen and her cubs at Ranscombe, to the 'Kingsbridge Gazette'. As a result of that publication I received one signed post card with a London address criticising me for supporting hunting and for killing a vixen and her cubs. I also received thirteen anonymous letters and post cards most of them signed 'sportswoman' or 'sportsman' from followers of our local Hunt, cursing and blasting me and calling down the wrath of all the Gods upon my head, wishing me the greatest ill-luck and ill-health they could muster, bitterly accusing me of destroying the sport of the people who had risked their lives during the war, fighting to save the lives of killsports such as me. Hunt followers threatened to shoot me and to slit my throat from ear to ear. Not one of these self-signed and self-styled sportspeople possessed the courage to say these things to my face. I received two telephone calls from farmers that I knew, one threatened Michael — who was no more than a boy — and one threatened me. The intelligence of these hunting people must have been sub-zero for there was no shortage of foxes to hunt, in fact there were too many foxes to hunt. We were actually doing the hunt a favour.

I thought I had burned all of the anonymous letters, but two have since turned up. I now wish that I had kept them all for I could have shown the world the type of so-called human that goes a-hunting. I am sure I could have since recognised the writers of more than one of these anonymous letters. There were known to have been nine litters of fox cubs reared in Flear Valley the previous summer.

Farmer friends from Flear Valley — from Malston Mill to East Allington — asked me to arrange a fox shoot with the Fox Destruction Society before their lambing commenced. We had arranged for the shoot to be held on Monday. On the Wednesday before the Monday, I met the master of the local hunt and explained to him the wishes of the farmers of Flear Valley. I invited him to co-operate with them, to avoid as far as possible the hounds entering that area before the Monday so as not to drive the foxes away. This was a practice the hunt had previously been deliberately adopting when they learned of a pending fox shoot.

Unfortunately, or maybe fortunately, mumps put me to bed for several days. On the Saturday the hounds were planned to meet at Sorley Cross, instead of going to Sorley Cross they went straight to Flear Valley and spent the whole day there. The hunt did this to the farmers who had permitted the hunt to hunt freely over their land. This was a diabolical affront to their best friends.

Had I not been confined to bed, and had I known that the master of the hunt had deliberately taken the hounds to Flear Valley, I would have taken a gun to Flear Valley and shot some of their hounds. This would have raised a stink.

The very next time that I went to the cattle market, the hunt master, Mr John Cornish, one of the leading local farmers, left his bunch of hunting cronies, came straight to where I stood and held his hand out for me to shake.

I looked him in the eye and said 'You are the meanest and most unsporting man I have even met. You are the last person I would ever wish to shake hands with.'

At that time all the merchants in the area were afraid of stocking fox snares in case the hunting fraternity boycotted their businesses. I purchased many thousands of fox snares from Youngs of Musterton, Somerset, and distributed them among those farmers who needed them.

Quite by chance I met Mr Owen Steer, the secretary of the Fox Destruction Society, as he left the office of his agricultural merchant employer. I said 'Owen, you certainly brewed up some trouble for me when you reported me as having killed a vixen and her cubs at Ranscombe.' Owen said 'You are not the only one who is in trouble. You must read this letter.' The letter was from one of his employer's customers who not only dared Owen to put another foot on his property, but also warned Owen's employer that if he did not sack Owen he would withdraw his custom from Owen's employer.

Owen said 'As a matter of fact, I have just been on the carpet over this letter. My employer wanted to know what I was doing acting as secretary for the Fox Destruction Society. I said to my employer, as you already know I keep over 2,000 laying hens and I stand to lose a considerable amount of money when foxes get amongst them, which foxes have already done. It is my life.' Owen's employer supported Owen's involvement with the society and refused to sack him.

A couple of years later I asked Owen if many of his employer's hunting customers had withdrawn their custom. Owen told me that 23 hunting people had withdrawn their custom from his employer.

The strife between the hunting people and the Fox Destruction Society, and between the hunting people and myself, had reached a stage when I said to myself 'It is time that someone put a stop to this nonsense.' It came about that on the first hunting day after Boxing Day, the hounds were due to meet at Sorley Cross. I had inspected my snares in the morning of that day, and had caught a fox which I had killed.

Evelyn's brothers Ernest and Frank were staying with us. Michael had obtained his driving licence. I said 'Come on boys, we are going for a drive. Michael can drive.' I placed the fox in the boot of the car. We timed ourselves to arrive at 11 a.m. and Michael stopped the car at the cross. I got out of the car, opened the boot, and threw the fox among the hounds. I shouted to the huntsman 'Blood the b − − − − −s Ronald, blood the b − − − − −s.' Ronald wasn't such a bad old stick really, it wasn't his fault.

The following Sunday, one whole column on the front page of one of the national Sunday papers was devoted to the fella who had the audacity to throw a dead fox among a pack of hounds. This was sacrilege. This adverse publicity brought the Masters of Foxhounds Association into the fray. Our local hunt was ordered to toe the line, and was ordered to stop provoking its best friends. That action brought the fox war to an end.

The snares soon appeared openly for sale in the shops. Hunting people were seen setting these snares themselves and gradually neighbours commenced speaking to each other again. Had there been one large respected squire in the area to influence the hunting people, the fox war would never have started. Small squires were two a penny in the area at the time. This was the first experience these little squires had of fox hunting and they were not equal to the occasion.

In fairness to the hunt, it could never be accused of being deliberately cruel. It would never permit hounds to kill a fox if it could be avoided. If it bred a good hound that would stick to the trail, it would be shot.

The more experienced foxes led the hunt a merry dance.

These old foxes would lay a false trail on one side of a valley and watch hounds from the other side of the valley. If hunting was stopped granny and granfer fox would have no exciting stories to pass on to their grandchildren of when and how they foxed the huntsman and the hounds.

It might be interesting to recall that it has been proven that foxes and badgers possess an acute sense of smell. Foxes can scent from long distances the fluids which a cow and a ewe discharge before they calve or lamb. When a sitting domestic fowl, or a sitting wild fowl, or a sitting bird from all or any species, rises when its eggs begin to hatch, to permit its chicks to move freely and to dry, this permits the strong odour of the steaming hatching eggs and the strong odour of the addled eggs to be carried on the breeze to be detected by foxes and by badgers at a considerable distance.

Hatching time is the most vulnerable time for all species of fowl and of birds. Where rabbits are a plague, badgers can be the farmer's best friend in keeping the number of rabbits in check. Nests of newly born rabbits are vulnerable to the scent, and possibly also to the hearing of badgers. I once counted 23 rabbits' nests which had contained newly-born rabbits, which had recently been dug up from the top of a field bank over a distance of less then 150 metres.

After myxomatosis had taken its toll, badgers killed and ate most if not all of the hedgehogs on this farm. The badgers usually dug a large hole to the centre of the hedge to reach the hedgehog. The hedgehog skin was left by the hole entrance.

Sentiment, sympathy and compassion are non-existent in nature. Badgers have been blamed for killing newly-born lambs, usually by pro-fox hunting people. From my considerable experience, while I can see no reason why badgers should not kill lambs, all that I can say is that it has never been proved to my satisfaction that badgers have ever killed a single lamb.

A mature badger is more than a match for any dog in a badger's home or set and while dogs are sometimes cut up badly by badgers, no dog has ever inflicted as much as a bruise on a mature badger when it has been attacked in its home or set. Brock reigns supreme in his underground castle, it is the dog who needs the sympathy. If and when a badger is dispatched humanely, digging them out with dogs can be one of the most humane ways of controlling their numbers.

There has been far too much emotive involvement in badger affairs by people who have never as much as seen a badger. It is the badgers who will suffer from this over-emotive involvement.

There is nothing that my family would like better than to possess a tame badger. Unfortunately they also possess fleas. We do know badgers give birth to their young within a short period of time at the beginning of February each year. It has been claimed that a badger's gestation period can vary considerably in length of time for the embryo to develop at the required speed to mature at this precise period of the year.

When we came here 48 years ago, there were 12 coveys of partridges on the farm. It has been some years since we saw the last one and skylarks appear to have gone the same way as the partridge. We can only guess what part the fox, the badger and the mink explosion played in their disappearance. All we do know is that these two events coincided.

Any bird that roosts, or lays its eggs, or hatches its chicks on the ground, is vulnerable. When I was young we kept a couple of hen turkeys which sometimes we took to a stag turkey to mate. One mating usually produced fertile eggs for as long as she kept laying. When we sat her to hatch out her turkey chicks during late July or August, she would often take her chicks away in the fields, when we would not see her for several days and sometimes weeks. Her chicks would thrive on insects they found in the hedges.

We learned to club rats to death from an early age after first catching them in gins, or when ricks were being threshed. Our sheepdogs and terriers were in their elements catching rats at threshing time. They would sometimes become very tired and rats would bite their faces and tongues. I have seen blood streaming down a dog's tongue from rat bites.

During the present winter around 400 tons of corn and around 500 tonnes of potatoes have been stored on the premises. A family of stoats have occupied the buildings and have annihilated the rats. It is strange that no-one raised a voice in protest when rats are clubbed to death, yet life is as sweet to the rat as it is to the fox, badger, mink, stoat, or to the human. Humans are completely illogical and unpredictable in their fantasies.

From clubbing rats we progressed to clubbing rabbits, sometimes with steel gins and sometimes with ferret and nets. The steel gin was a barbarous implement, it maimed and it killed all manner and all types of bird and small mammal, yet without the assistance of this steel gin to keep the rabbit population under control the human inhabitants of this small island would have all starved to death. The rabbit population might have been controlled by baiting them with poisoned carrots, or they might have been gassed in their burrows. They could not have been kept under control by ferreting them for rabbits will only bolt well under certain weather conditions. When they do not bolt, ferrets will eat their eyes out and the rabbits will starve to death.

During the middle of the 1930's when I arrived home late one night, I picked up a twelve bore gun, eighteen cartridges and a torch, and proceeded on my motor cycle to Kilquite which at the time was unoccupied. I entered the field behind the house and fired at the first rabbit that I saw, I bowled it over but it picked itself together and ran into a hole. I followed it and as it turned to look out of the hole, I caught it by a front foot but I lost my grip and it got away. With the seventeen cartridges remaining I shot seventeen rabbits.

On the strength of that achievement, I went to a Mr Creber of Menheniot and purchased 1,500 cartridges. The following evening Hedley and I went shooting with the torch. We finished up with 80 rabbits that night. We walked to the top of the knoll in Meladrim Field and standing on one spot Hedley shot 18 rabbits as fast as he could reload his gun. The rabbits had squatted and as I moved the torch an eye would glisten sufficiently to betray the position of the rabbit. Between us we soon fired off the 1,500 cartridges.

Then Leonard Rowe, for five shillings, sold me a fawn-coloured nestlebird bitch from a litter of greyhound pups. I named her Pippa, or Pip and I obtained a powerful car headlamp which I attached to a six volt battery. One evening she caught and retrieved 70 rabbits to me. I took her out again the following evening, when she retrieved her twentieth rabbit which she placed at my feet and looked up appealingly at me, instead of holding it up for me to take. Her look spoke volumes, the rabbit ran away. She had had enough. I stroked her and caressed her, then took her straight home.

The strong car headlamp that we used with the dog would hold wood-pigeons in its beam to shoot when they flew out of their roosting trees. The estate gamekeepers could not be expected to relish the new trend in their tenant's rabbiting activities, with so many pheasants roosting in the trees, and with so many guns banging off at night. One could quite easily sympathise with them. During winter nights 30 hen pheasants could be seen roosting in low apple trees growing beside the path through the orchard that we regularly traversed to reach the cattle sheds. To me this was a pleasant sight. I was never tempted to take one, they did not belong to me.

Over 5,000 rabbits were killed on Molenick Farm each year. A considerable amount of my time had been taken up with killing rabbits, with killing vermin to protect growing crops, and in treating farm animals to ease their suffering by feeding them well, then by helping cows and ewes to deliver their calves and their lambs, treating sheep that were afflicted with that terrible and painful scourge footrot, frequently treating sheep that had been attacked with maggots, preventing birds from picking out the eyes of sheep and pulling out the sheep's intestines while the sheep was alive, and treating cattle, sheep, horses and pigs with their many and varied ailments. A large part of my life has been devoted to fighting nature, and nature's abiding cruelties as humanely as I know how, mainly to ensure my own survival but also to ensure the survival of humans in general.

I once witnessed a buzzard sweep to pick up a young live rabbit in its talons to fly to a gatepost where it perched to leisurely skin the rabbit alive before eating it. I witnessed another buzzard swoop on a full grown partridge to sever its neck instantly, I drove the buzzard off to collect the partridge, which we ate.

Approaching the entrance to Charliecombe Field one day I was attracted to the screams of a rabbit, which emanated from the lane hedge. I crept quietly towards the field gate, screening myself from the view of several other rabbits feeding in the same field along by the hedge.

I peered through the space between the gatepost and the hedge, while the rabbit continued to scream. The rabbit duly emerged from the hedge to proceed some distance out into the field, where it crouched still screaming. I then observed a stoat emerge from the hedge to follow the same path as the screaming rabbit, in the process jumping over rabbits that were feeding in the field. The screaming rabbit remained crouched, immobilised with fear, it remained immobile while the stoat sucked its lifeblood from its neck.

It was along the bottom of Charliecombe Field at a later date that I counted 23 rabbits nests over a distance of 150 metres which had been dug out and destroyed by badgers. These 23 nests would have contained more than 100 young rabbits.

I have found snipes frozen to death from their beak becoming trapped in fast-freezing mud while they were searching for food. We are told that not a sparrow falleth to the ground but that our Heavenly Father knoweth, so God would also know about the rabbits and the snipe, but how does God's knowledge help the sparrows, the rabbits, or the snipe?

There are many happenings relating to nature which are attributed to God's creation, which are past my understanding.

Last evening Trevor called in to say that the previous evening he had found one of his ewes on her back where birds had cleanly pecked out one of the ewe's eyes. Trevor had put the ewe on her feet, and she appeared sufficiently strong and capable of coping with her two lambs. Last evening he discovered this ewe on her back again, birds had pecked the ewe's other eye out.

This is happening somewhere every day where sheep are kept. Sheep's skin itches beneath the fleece of wool, sheep roll over to relieve the irritation when they become trapped on their backs by their fleeces or by uneven ground surfaces, when they become easy prey for these birds. Wherever sheep are kept during hot summer weather, many will be attacked by maggots and many will be eaten alive.

Electricity came to Cornish towns soon after the First World War, followed by electrically-propelled labour-saving gadgets in the home and in industry.

Before the arrival of the incubator, eggs from domesticated and wild fowl were incubated and fostered in the natural way by the layers of the eggs or by broody domesticated hens. The incubation period for the various species of most small fowl was around 21 days, while thicker-shelled eggs from Guinea fowl, turkeys and most species of water fowl took about a week longer. Most species of fowl carry fleas which cause them much annoyance and distress, especially when incubating eggs during warm weather. Hens will sometimes leave their eggs if fleas are not dealt with.

Gamekeepers incubated pheasant eggs under hens in specially-made nest boxes and hens were lifted from their eggs every day, tethered by a leg, fed and watered.

When Charlie Jane was gamekeeper for Pentille Estate he found a hen standing on her eggs when he went to feed her. He took her out, wrung her neck and said 'There, you vermint, if you won't sit you shan't stand.'

Mrs Alford renowned for her successes when showing dressed poultry at Christmas Fatstock Shows tested four goose eggs with warm water for signs of life. They had been incubated by a hen sitting on a hedge just before the eggs were due to hatch. As she found no life in the eggs she smashed them against a nearby wall. Then she placed four fresh eggs under the same hen. Drawn by the smell of the smashed addled eggs a fox ate the hen the following night.

Electricity also produces its hazards. One of Trevor's tractors caught fire and burned out in recent years while working in a barn, the barn remained undamaged.

Another tractor caught fire while standing idle in a shed measuring 105' × 105' containing hay, straw and corn. Fortunately Norman, a neighbour, observed the tractor burning as he was passing the shed. After the fire had been extinguished the tractor was removed from the shed. During the same year, one of Norman's tractors caught fire and burned out during the night while standing idle in the yard. These three fires originated from the electrical systems, and Trevor now removes terminals from batteries when tractors are left standing idle in sheds.

While my mother had been a deeply religious person, she did not ram religion down the throats of anyone. She taught by example. She was a person one could converse and reason with. Before and during my mother's time, before the scientific advance in the knowledge and in the understanding of the structure of the human being, and physical procreation as recognised at the present time, it had been commonly assumed that abnormalities in babies were caused by, or were the result of, the mother having been frightened while carrying the baby in her womb.

When quite young I heard my mother say that the mother of a certain abnormal child must have been frightened by something when carrying the child. I said 'Mum, while fright or shock might cause a mother to abort her child, I would have thought it would have taken more than a fright to alter the composition of an embryo once the embryo had been formed.' My mother said 'Then what causes these abnormalities in children?' I said 'Mother, some child abnormalities might be caused by hereditary flaws, or hereditary weaknesses in the parent's physical or mental structure, which would certainly become enhanced when a child had been inbred. We must understand that the chemical anatomy of an animal, including the human, is delicate, intricate, amazing. It would be surprising if every inter dependent part of the body structure of a child always functioned normally. An occasional flaw in an individual's anatomy is to be expected. The structure of the body of an animal, or plant, is equally amazing. Life within the animal body or animal or plant is overwhelmingly incomprehensible and inimitable. Whereas cruel nature maintains its health, strength and vigour from the survival of the fittest only, among humans the advance in natural science has produced the survival of those with hereditary flaws and the unhealthy, weak, and the listless to procreate. Healthwise, this is reducing the human animal to a second class inhabitant of the earth. Since that chat with my mother sixty five years ago, the science of anatomy and procreation has advanced considerably. It is now known and accepted that physical reproduction can be upset by many things, including misuse of drugs, nutrient imbalance and disease.

Modern technology and modern science together have eradicated some killer diseases, but others are constantly arriving to replace them. From where do the killer diseases originate?

Trewashford Farm was poorly served with piped spring water. Large Delabole slates were bolted together to form large static tanks to collect rainwater from the roofs of the farm buildings. These tanks were drained and cleaned every autumn, yet by the following autumn these static rainwater tanks were teeming with marine life, which were mainly red in colour darting hither and thither. How, why or where did this marine life originate?

Dr Jeffrey Harris of Strathclyde University told the British Association in Glasgow earlier this year that tests on diamonds from the Kimberley mines in South Africa showed that the diamonds were 3,140 million years old. Listening to the radio while driving a car the same afternoon a voice said 'Life as we know it has not been in existence for more than 480,000 years.' Some time later while watching a programme on Africa, the speaker, a professor, said that human life had existed in Africa for 2,000,000 years and that Christianity had existed there a million years before it came to England. And there was I believing that Christianity had arrived with Christ a mere 2,000 years ago. What should we believe?

As a young, innocent child, I was taught that there was a Heaven and a Hell, and that it was only the good people who went to Heaven when they died, and that all the bad people went to Hell and spent Eternity in a fiery furnace. In my innocence I had believed what I had been taught. Consequently, more than once I cried myself to sleep in sympathy for the bad people who would be spending Eternity in this fiery furnace.

Having grown up, having come face to face with nature and with the realities of life, and having compared the Scriptures with nature I felt humiliated that in my innocence these Christians had made a monkey out of me. I have never completely forgiven these Christian fanatics.

Having lived with and having studied nature for 83 years, having lived with and having studied human behaviour for 83 years, having concluded that conception, birth, life and death is a gigantic lottery for all living creatures great and small, and while it can be accepted that God can exist in the mind of the believer, it is almost impossible in the face of logic to believe that God exists anywhere outside the mind of the believer.

Believers now claim and declare that no matter how wicked a human has been in this life, all that he or she has to do to enter heaven is to repent of his or her misdeeds. In this context Hitler and as many of his henchmen who had repented of their misdeeds before they died would have been welcomed in heaven as good and faithful servants, to sit by God's right hand, while the many victims of their wickedness would have died before they had an opportunity of repenting and would automatically, presumably have been condemned to eternal damnation in the next world.

Also in this context it is a sobering thought that while an estimated 150,000 human foetuses (one for every five live births) will be deliberately aborted in this country during 1985, Members of Parliament who sanctioned these abortions, the parents or the parent of the foetus, the doctors and the nurses who performed the abortions, will presumably enter heaven to sit by the right hand of God, with the foetus they have aborted, if they also repent before they die.

This philosophy raises the pertinent and the fundamental question of 'justice'. Is there any justice at all in this world?

It should not be in the least surprising that only 15% of adults in this country are members of a Christian church. The Christian faith is only one of many religious faiths. Probably less than one per cent of the world's population are followers of the Christian faith. Is this also surprising? It has been claimed that the Islamic faith has a larger following than the Christian faith.

During 1983 there were 393,000 marriages and 175,000 divorces in this country. Earthly possessions, or the lack of earthly possessions, directly or indirectly influences the number of aborted foetuses and the number of divorces in this country. Doctors and nurses perform these abortions only because they are being paid. If a guilty party exists of a divorce was required by law to forfeit his or her financial rights in a marriage we would observe fewer broken homes.

If it is moral, considerate, sharing, good living citizens of which the world is so desperately in need, it is more likely to come from the example of a moral unbroken family life, free and devoid of hypocrisy, cant and humbug, where affection and consideration for others is the norm, than from the combined bible-punching.

This country is regarded as being one of the most favoured in which to be born. Even so, the commoners, the workers who are the backbone and the wealth of this country are being conned and exploited by the church, by the state, by the financiers, by the exploiters and by the media from the cradle to the grave. We have already looked at the church, let us now examine the state. While our Members of Parliament might have been democratically elected, that is where democracy ends. This country is run by dictatorship with the Party Whips enforcing this dictatorship. Not until the Party Whips are abolished will this country become a democracy. Members of Parliament are elected by their constituents to represent their constituency not their party. Every bill that is presented to the House should be voted in or out on its merits on a free vote of the house, in the interest of the country at large, not in the interests of any one party.

In the House at the present time a war is being waged between the Right and the Left at the expense of the centre, the happy medium where Government should emanate. For too long the minority Government in power has been so intent on feathering its own members' nests that an imbalance of wealth has taken place. With rich getting richer and the poor getting poorer. Between 1979 and 1993 this country has been governed by one party with an electoral support of 40%, this has meant that almost 60% of the electorate of this country has not been represented in Parliament with disastrous consequences. The welfare of this country is too important for any one party to govern. At the present time the electorate voters consist of 40% Conservative, 40% Labour and 20% Liberal.

A Parliamentary session should be for a fixed time of four or five years. The most important person in any business or venture is its leader, so the Prime Minister should be elected by the whole House regardless of which party he represents. Each party should be permitted to present bills in the House by rotation based on its electoral support. At the present time this would amount to two for the Conservatives, two for Labour and one for the Liberals. In this way over 90% of the electorate would be represented in Parliament, against about 40% now. Every member of the House should vote on his conscience and the merits of the bill and without the Party Whips breathing down his neck. This would be more likely to ensure that the right measures were being adopted. In any case this would be democracy at its best. This would eliminate the need for the present dubious proportional reform, and would abolish the present disgusting behaviour in the House which is portrayed daily on television. How can we expect discipline in the streets when we see so much indiscipline in the Houses of Parliament. There is no place in a democracy for secret societies. They inevitably invite suspicion, whether justified or not. Freemasons have frequently claimed that they have nothing to hide. It is for this very reason that I invite every one of them to write a small 'M' behind their name wherever it appears. I also invite all non-Masons to place a small 'z' for zero where necessary. Finances are an essential part of any and every business concern. It is nevertheless, a hard pill for the low paid workers to see multi-millionaires spring up over night. They may rightly ask what strings these wealthy few have pulled or what massive favours received. Who have they exploited to become so fortunate overnight? Is it because the low paid worker has not been represented for fourteen years in the Government? The low paid worker is being exploited right, left and centre, more especially by the professionals. Take Mr Meat, the butcher from Helston in Cornwall, who when working in his shop saw a dog enter his shop and snatch and run off with a chunk of beef. He hastily followed the dog to a house not far away belonging to a Mr Cabbage, a solicitor. He asked to see Mr Cabbage and was ushered into his office. Mr Cabbage asked Mr Meat what he could do for him. Mr Meat said, 'If a dog entered my shop and stole a piece of beef would I have claim on the owner?' Mr Cabbage said, 'Of course.' Mr Meat said, 'The dog was yours. I want five pounds, please.'

Mr Cabbage said, 'Here's the five pounds. Now I want fifty pounds.' Mr Meat said, 'What for?' Mr Cabbage answered, 'For professional advice.' That man was no cabbage.

There was another similar case: Two chaps who were walking the Helford river when they spied an oyster. Both dived and seized the oyster together. Each claimed to have seen it first. They both argued the ownership. Neither would give in so they decided to go to the nearest solicitor and settle the dispute. With both clutching the oyster they reached his office and explained their case. The solicitor said, 'I must first take charge of the oyster.' They handed it over. The solicitor took out his pocket knife opened the oyster and swallowed it, handing back one shell to each. 'There,' said the solicitor, 'that will be fifty pounds.'

Now Jethro, he do come from Cornwall too, but as I do know 'e were born out Buryan way 'e was.

I was sitting talking to Mr George Martin in his office at Liskeard Cattle Market when a man standing at the door said, 'Excuse me, would you be a Tucker?' I said, 'Who is enquiring?' He answered, 'Joe Speare.' I recollected, 'My Uncle Edmund married a Kate Speare.' He said, 'She was my cousin. Aunt Kate who had passed away more than forty years ago and Uncle Edmund twenty five years ago.' I visited Joe who lived at Redgate, St Cleer and spent many happy hours with him and his wife Edna. Not long after this, one morning, he awoke and realised he was blind, and not many months after, he lost his hearing, but he survived these hardships for quite a few years with a devoted wife to care for him. Many times perfect strangers have asked me, 'You baint a Tucker, be 'e?' Our family appear to possess a distinctive voice. One Sunday, several years after we had moved into Devon, Chris

Speare of Horrabridge, formerly of Bolus Flemming, took my family and me to Meldon Dam in Devon for a summer picnic. The following morning the telephone rang and the voice enquired if I had been to this particular picnic spot the previous day because his sister Beatrice had also been there and, on returning home had told him that a 'Tucker' had been there. When asked what 'Tucker' she replied that she did not know. She had only heard him, she hadn't actually seen him. After Gran had died, when this Beatrice left school she became housekeeper to my three bachelor uncles at Bealbury for several years until she married and became Mrs Rickard of St Dominick.

That was by the way, now to return to the subject of confidence tricks and exploitation when we are offered something free, remember that there are not many things in this life that are completely free, except the air we breathe. Everything has to be paid for by someone. Time and space are maybe the only things that are endless.

The professional gardeners are trying to exploit when they preach to us of the benefits of organic produced food. Garden compost, farmyard manure, and town soil contain disease, fungi, harmful bacteria and toxins, animal by-products such as blood and bone carry diseases, at the same time condemning the use of bag fertilisers. What are the facts? Phosphates, potash and nitrogen are the main plant foods. Lime is used to activate the bacteria in the soil which turns vegetation into plant food. An excess of lime in the soil is detrimental because it locks up certain minerals and trace elements. Rock phosphate, basic slag, the various potashes, and lime, are all mined, they are situated in condensed form in various parts of the world. They do not contain weed seed, disease, fungi, harmful bacteria or toxins. They are neither chemical or artificial, they are the same plant nutrients that already exist in the soil. Nitrogen produces bulk. Nitrogen exists in the air we breathe. What are these professional gardeners trying to prove? It is generally accepted that garden compost produces humus, a friable tilth and a moist seed, but it is not so well-known that lime activates the bacteria which converts vegetation with plant food, which also produces a moist seed bed. Soil will dry out quickly if there is a deficiency of lime. If there were no bag fertilisers sown we would all starve. I have been unable to discover who it is these professional gardeners are trying to convince (apart from themselves). Are these gardeners reading the wrong books? Or is it a case of over-education confusing the mind? It is these so-called professionals who are at the present time making such a 'hash' of their trades.

And now to the Common Market: What is there which is in common between the nations of this market? Not language, only greed.

In spite of all that has gone before, British subjects still retain some rapport, perhaps it is a latent kinship, or simply a healthy respect for each other with the German people. Also Norway is compatible with the British subjects, but that is the limit of the market's friendship.

When I voted in the referendum in the early seventies to join Europe I was under the impression that this would stop all future European wars. I had seen so much anguish caused by war that I was willing to sacrifice wealth for peace. Twenty years later I am forced to accept that peace is not on the E.E.C. agenda. Their agenda is concerned only with expanding wealth and as we should all by now know, pursuit of wealth is the road to disaster.

In Britain we have Scotland and Wales objecting to being ruled from London, with some justification. Britain is now being ruled from Brussels, where rules and regulations are being churned out by the ream. Some necessary, many unnecessary. We do not know where we stand on farming and we are probably unwittingly breaking the law, thereby becoming criminals every other day of our lives. Farming has been compelled to dispose of one of its finest assets, the Milk Marketing Board, because it is a monopoly business while the expensive Water, Gas Telephone and Electricity Boards are permitted to continue. After all, milk is produced at less than a third of the cost of beer. It seems bizarre that farmers are not permitted to cost a product and ask a reasonable profit on or a price tag on his work. He is expected to accept whatever the buyer is prepared to offer him.

A CONCLUDING RESUME:

The facts of life. But what is life? Life is a brief chance encounter with the weird, wonderful, terribly cruel world of nature.

For some life will be good, for some it will be a struggle, and for some it will be Hell. It will depend largely on the station in life of one's parents. Speaking generally: Conception, birth, life and death is a gigantic lottery for all living things. Every human arrives on this Earth planet by chance, whether conceived inside of wedlock or outside. From the countless acorns produced by the mighty oak over perhaps hundreds of years it takes but one acorn to produce a second mighty oak. Likewise, it takes but one fertilized human egg among the countless human eggs produced to create another human. It would appear that wherever there is a beginning there is the inevitable end.

It might also be reasonable to assume that there was indeed a beginning to all things. The Bible claims that God made all things that was made which presumably included this planet Earth, the countless other planets and suns in the countless galaxies that exist out in the cosmos. The Old Testament of the Bible contains the history of the Jewish race: who begot whom, and who fought and killed whom, written and created by Jews with a limited knowledge of this planet Earth or of the unknown troubles that existed at the time, all of which had created their own Gods to worship. Of the thousand and one Gods that humans on this planet worship, what leads followers of the Old Testament to claim, or to believe, that theirs is the one and only true religion, or the true God.

The ten commandments are, of course, acceptable rules to me for leading a good life. Jesus is alleged to have added two more, 'Love one another.' 'Sell all thou hast and give it to the poor.' Nevertheless, 'Thou shalt not kill.' is a strange commandment coming from God, when every animal predator including the human will, during its lifetime, kill and consume up to one thousand innocent, defenceless creatures to maintain their own survival. These victims treasure their life the same as the predators. Where killing is concerned the history of the church of this country, and the history of mankind causes an offensive, putrid atmosphere that irritates any right thinking soul.

In spite of the many religions that exist throughout the world or because of so many religions, the twentieth century must have witnessed more horrors than any previous time for, we have been informed that there are twenty four wars being raged around the world at the present time. The church can be frequently seen begging to pay for one or another restoration scheme for a church or a cathedral. When asked for a reason the ultimate answer is to 'Glory Mankind'. The sympathy of Jesus is with the poor. Jesus did not need to build massive cathedrals to preach His gospel and he drove the worshippers out of the temple, and probably would do so again if he ever returned. I have listened to many parables of the Prodigal Son preached by so called educated theologians that have left me puzzled. It seems an earthly father may lay out the red carpet and kill the fatted calf, and forgive him, only if his Prodigal Son had sown his wild oats in a foreign country completely unknown to his father's neighbours.

The Parable of the Talents is also confusing, I have observed that the nicest people are those that possess the fewest Talents. They were content with the few that they possessed and did not covet others. 'Why take away the few Talents that they already possessed?'

About three years ago I was sitting beside a local Methodist preacher in an Anglican church, when the vicar came over to speak. I do not remember how the situation came about but I did question how Jesus came to rise on the third day, having died on a Friday afternoon about four o'clock and yet met and spoke to Mary Magdalene early on the Sunday morning about forty hours after He was alleged to have died. That, I had considered had been the second day. OH! They gave me such a rollicking for questioning the Bible, so I said no more. They were two delightful people but, why are they, as Christians, so 'touchy' and apprehensive when discussing the Bible with others.

I was born into a Christian family. Consequently, because of this, I was indoctrinated (brain washed) into a Christian faith from an early age. The answer is for the Glorification of God, but in fact it's for the glorification of the church. Anyone who will believe that will believe anything. I do not possess the Talents to understand these teachings, maybe I am one of those who should be deprived of the few Talents now possessed.

By and large, one's religion and beliefs will follow the same example as one's parents, regardless of logic or common sense. This lack of thought and sense permits hatred and strife to flourish between religions. Man's inhumanity to man is more evident in mankind than within or between any other animal species. Rarely in life on this planet is anything straightforward, either black or white, and there is always two sides to any subject.

Rarely, after discussion, will any answer be complete or satisfactory to both sides. What is so objectional about theologians and the Church is that they believe their theories and answers are absolutely correct, which must not be disputed by anyone. The main theme of theologians and the Church is that 'God is Love', but what is God and what is love? Nature in all its beauty, in all its slendour, in all its bounty, trauma, anguish, pathos, pain, suffering and terror is the only living God. Humans still worship other Gods which include, wealth, power, corruption, sex, self, art, music, singing, architecture, preditors, also the landscape beauty, wetlands and arid lands, also the sun that evaporates water to create clouds, later falling as rain, which is the only visible creator and sustainer of life on this planet. The Gods that humans worship are endless. 'LOVE' is the most misused and abused word in the English language. This abuse has cheapened its real meaning to the state that it is almost worthless. Its present use by the Church and by novelists is an insult to the basic meaning. The only love that can be found in Nature is parental love dominated by maternal love. When did anyone ever observe the Church sacrifice for the cause? Not until the Church follows the example set by the Salvation Army will its influence ever be for the good of mankind. The parable of the lost sheep is a clear example of the Church hierarchy which is not at all concerned with the lost sheep, but only with administering to those within the fold who, hopefully, will contribute to their coffers. The Old Testament consists of books written and produced by various individuals. It is based on their beliefs. The story of Adam and Eve has become outdated and no longer able to compete with modern knowledge. I am more concerned with the psalmist who wrote those beautiful psalms especially the twenty third 'The Lord is my Shepherd. I shall not want.' etc. If the psalmist did possess immense wealth and his four hundred wives and five hundred concubines he was in a perfect position to write these words but, could his eunuchs be expected to believe these words also? How naive can humans be? What do we know about the New Testament? If God sent Jesus into this world to redeem the world, God should have arranged for Jesus to have written His own Gospel message, and not to have left it for the others to write. The alleged Gospel of Jesus was sufficiently credible without the need to dramatise His birth, His resurrection and His ascension. Christianity appears to have been founded upon sentiment, fantasy, fear of the church, God, the unknown. Sentiment and fantasy have nothing in common with the true facts of life and the true facts of nature while sermons and prayers inspired and consoled countless indoctorinated believers throughout the ages. They are little if anything more than a clever manipulation of foundationless and unsubstantiated words, upon a need to justify the existence of the universe and of mankind, upon a need to solve the unsolvable mysteries of life. The human race, the most cruel amongst the many animal species. It kills not only to eat to survive, it kills and maims for sport and for spite. It kills for greed and for profit, for jealousy, lust, and selfishness. It kills the 'Jesus's' and 'Martin Luther King's' of this world. Our actual knowledge of Jesus is limited. Contrary to what we are led to believe, we do not know where or when Jesus was born. We do not know anything about Jesus from the age of twelve years for a period of over twenty years. All we know is that if we followed the example of the alleged teachings of Jesus, the world would be a much safer and more pleasant place in which to live. The basis for living a happy, contented, carefree life is simple and effective, it is living with truthfulness, honesty, integrity, fidelity, sobriety, tolerance, and the ability to accept defeat gracefully. There are many who already follow the example set by Jesus who do not 'claim' to be Christians, but should be known to serve under a different banner, just to shame the greedy, selfish, rich establishment rhetoric of insincere, out of touch with nature, out of touch with the facts of life, theologians.

Wherever there is a beginning, there is the inevitable end. This is the end of this book. While we may not have discovered from whence and where we came or whither we goest we can at least rest assured that whatever trials and tribulations we have experienced in this life:

EPITOME

There'll be no more diggin'
No more scrapin'
No more askin'
And No refusin'
There'll be green, green pastures
Barns full and plenty
Round the bend of the road.

Another theory put forward is that this planet Earth was created or had originated some five billion years ago, and will last another five billion years, by which time the sun will have burned itself out.

Yet another theory is that life originated on this Earth about two hundred years ago.

If these theories are correct, one must ask the question, where was God during the intervening five billion years. The simple truth is, that while life appears in a multitude of forms, shapes, and sizes, in a multitude of profound, intricate and amazing organisms, and in a multitude of beautiful colours, the origin of this planet

Earth and its myriads of living organisms has been lost in the depth of time and will remain lost in the depth of time for ever, but this will not deter humans from theorising and guessing.

We now know that individual fertilised human embryos occasionally naturally divide to produce or to create identical twins.

We now also know that provided it takes place between the first and the eighth day after the embryo has been fertilised, a human embryo can be physically divided and become naturally sub-divided to produce or to create 2, 3 or 4 living embryos which can develop and mature into 2, 3 or 4 individual independent identical human beings.

While I am unable to understand from whence, from where or how life originates to enter and to inhabit the original human embryo, and the divided and the sub-divided embryos, believers still claim and insist the Bible contains and can produce all the answers relating to creation.